How Else Will They Know

Passing on the Faith
to the
Next Generation

ROD ZWEMKE

How Else Will They Know

How Else Will They Know

FOREWORD by Jay McSwain

When my friend Rod asked me to write the forward for *How Else Will They Know?* I was thrilled and elated for numerous reasons. First, right after I started reading, I realized that what Rod had written were timeless principles from God's Word, but said in a fresh way that I had never seen written in any book. Secondly, the first day I began reading I read the principle – God as priority – and the importance of observing the Sabbath as a family, which generated a conversation with my 20-year-old daughter. She was in the process of transferring to the University of Georgia and would be finding a new church to call home. The insights gleaned from just the first principle were immediately put into practice by me with my daughter. Thirdly, I am part of a mentoring group in which the men collectively have 11 children of various age ranges. The insights from these men on how we can live out the principles in *As for Me and My House* were beyond words to describe. I know if you read this book with others, their observations, experience, and ideas will be invaluable to you.

Finally, I want to recommend that you read this book not only for the simple, but profound insights written in a fresh way, but for who wrote the book. I know many who read *As for Me and My House* may never meet Rod Zwemke. I have known Rod since before he was married and watched him and his wife, Gabrian, live out the principles taught in this book with their three children. I rarely use the word anointed to describe someone. With the previous said I believe Rod has been anointed by God to write *How Else Will They Know?* His example to me and many others and his ability to share these principles in a way that can be immediately implemented will bring about transformation in your family's life if lived out as I have seen Rod live them out through the years in his family.

How Else Will They Know

How Else Will They Know

CONTENTS

How Else Will They Know

ACKNOWLEDGMENTS

SCRIPTURES TAKEN FROM THE HOLY BIBLE, NEW INTERNATIONAL VERSION®, NIV®. COPYRIGHT © 1973, 1978, 1984, 2011 BY BIBLICA, INC.™ USED BY PERMISSION OF ZONDERVAN. ALL RIGHTS RESERVED WORLDWIDE. WWW.ZONDERVAN.COM THE "NIV" AND "NEW INTERNATIONAL VERSION" ARE TRADEMARKS REGISTERED IN THE UNITED STATES PATENT AND TRADEMARK OFFICE BY BIBLICA, INC.™

How Else Will They Know

1 Then it Hit Me

Near the Top

Let me begin by saying I love being a dad. I looked forward to being a dad most of my life. When I was 30 years old, we had our first child, a girl we named Addison. Then, seventeen months later, God blessed us with a boy, Dane. In the months that followed the arrival of child number two, my wife, Gabrian and I prayed that God would make clear to us both if we were to have another child. Twenty-one months later, we had our third, our daughter Shea. How's that for God answered prayer loud and clear?

So, in our early thirties, my wife and I went from being DINK WAD'S (dual income no kids, with a dog), to being parents of three preschoolers. It was a major lifestyle shift for both of us, not to mention Dory the dog (yeah, "Finding Nemo" was a big deal then). In addition to being a husband, a pastor, a friend, a co-worker, and other roles, now I had the added responsibility of being a parent. So, where would parenting fall in priority to all these other roles?

Short answer - near the top. Right after being a follower of God, and a husband to my wife, being dad comes in at a close third. That meant I not only needed to put my time and energy towards being a good dad, I also needed to have some idea on *how* to be a dad.

A Short List

My kids are now all teenagers, so before jumping ahead, let's hover around the preschool years. We were swimming in diapers, stuffed animals, and bodily fluids! As hard work as those years were, I miss them. I loved all the time I could spend holding, playing with, hugging, snuggling, and kissing my kids. Now I have to bribe them to give me a hug!

1

How Else Will They Know

It was in those days that I began to search for how God wanted me to raise my kids in a godly way. I read through the New Testament to give me a battle plan. With a notebook in hand, I was ready to fill pages with my findings. I settled in for a series of rich discoveries and specific descriptions on how to do this right. What I found surprised me. There simply wasn't much there in the way of instruction. The following is the short list of the verses that I found:

> *Fathers, do not exasperate your children; instead, bring them up in the training and instruction of the Lord. Ephesians 6:4*

> *Fathers, do not embitter your children, or they will become discouraged. Colossians 3:21*

> *Instead, we were like young children among you. Just as a nursing mother cares for her children, so we cared for you. Because we loved you so much, we were delighted to share with you not only the gospel of God but our lives as well. 1 Thessalonians 2:7–8*

> *For you know that we dealt with each of you as a father deals with his own children, encouraging, comforting and urging you to live lives worthy of God, who calls you into his kingdom and glory. 1 Thessalonians 2:11–12*

> *Moreover, we have all had human fathers who disciplined us and we respected them for it. How much more should we submit to the Father of spirits and live! Hebrews 12:9*

As I looked up from the page, I was dumbfounded. Seven verses? That's it?

How Else Will They Know

I knew that God had told us to make disciples of all nations. In Matthew 28:19 we are commanded to do that. That command includes us going to people outside the faith, leading them to Jesus, seeing them baptized and connected to a local church, and then teaching them to obey the commands of Jesus. Making disciples is something I've been actively pursuing much of my adult life. I was certain that God wanted me to intentionally invest in my children, like I had in other people over the years. I mean, why wouldn't He want me to do in my home what He has commanded me (and everyone) to do everywhere, in every nation, with every person? I am certain that God does want me to make disciples in my home, I just honestly thought that there would be more specific instructions on how to do that with my family.

As I poured back over these verses, I found some helpful nuggets. A summary of my findings from the list of verses above, includes the following:

- Don't be too harsh or demanding so that your kids become bitter because they never can please you
- Show love and care that is usually natural for a mother
- Provide emotional support to my kids in the form of encouragement, comfort and challenge that they might grow emotionally and spiritually
- Discipline my kids to honor and obey myself and their mother
- God expects the parent to teach their kids about Him, providing "training and instruction in the Lord"

That's really good, helpful stuff, but I wanted a plan. What I really wanted to know is what does this "training and instruction in the Lord" look like? I chewed on this apparent lack of direction for some time. Sure, I could wing it and hope for the best, but I really wanted to do this right. My prayer on and off over these months was for God to show me how to lead my family spiritually.

How Else Will They Know

Out of the Blue

I wish I could take credit for the idea that I got for living out the principles of this book, but to be honest, it would be disingenuous. I couldn't tell you where I was or what was on my mind when the thought hit me, but I can tell you that I was not thinking about anything pertaining to the topic of this book. Then, out of the blue the question hit me, "How did the Jewish people pass their faith along from generation to generation, from the time of Moses all the way past Jesus' day and even today?" Out of that spark of inspiration from God, the rest of what you will read flowed like a river through study, prayer, and the help of my friend Jeff. As we studied the scriptures, the thought took on life. When you stop to think about it, it is incredibly remarkable that the Jewish people have passed their faith along, generation to generation, for more than 4,000 years.

That would be an amazing feat in our modern world, but think about what they didn't have over the years. They didn't have any resources like books or fliers, or a printing press for that matter. They didn't have an internet to share best practices. For many of those years, the typical Jewish family would not own a copy of the scriptures in their home. If you and I feel ill equipped to lead our families, I couldn't imagine how these Jewish parents must have felt.

What *did* they have to teach their children about the God who loved them and wanted a relationship with them? What they had was a lifestyle of worshiping God through the practice of the Sabbath and the Jewish Festivals. Boom. That was it. These families had a pattern built into their yearly calendar to teach their children the faith. Their children saw their parents' worship. The child worshiped with their family, and learned about God through those experiences. Each of the festivals had a specific lesson to learn that could also be explained, grasped, and experienced by the children. They were lessons that they could see, touch, taste, smell and feel. This was not classroom learning, but life on life learning as the parents and the children celebrated together. This is exactly how children learn, which is why, when you want to teach anyone, concepts are good, but experiential learning is better. What we know now about childhood education is that kids learn best through experience, especially if being learned from a parent. Studies have shown that children are much more likely to copy their parents' actions rather than their words.[1] Here is God's plan for leading a family spiritually - you have shared experiences as a family seeking God together. You show them how to follow God. God's plan was and is genius!

As we unpack God's plan for the family as a place for spiritual growth and development, let me encourage you to use this book like a textbook. To use this resource properly, I encourage you to highlight and underline key thoughts in this book. I also encourage you to write your own ideas in the margins as you think about your own family. Use the space provided to write your answers to the questions provided at the end of each chapter. Basically, make a mess out of this book so that God can make something beautiful as you apply its principles. If you are reading this book in a digital format, make notes of your own or print it out so you too can capture your thoughts for your family. If you are listening to the audiobook version, take notes of your own to make the most of this experience.

Early and Often

Even as early as the creation account, we see that God had in mind the festivals. And God said, "Let there be lights in the vault of the sky to separate the day from the night, and let them serve as signs to mark sacred times, and days and years…" (Genesis 1:14) God placed the sun and the moon exactly as He wanted them so that He could mark the festivals for us. Each year, a rhythm of worship is established in the lives of those who practice the festivals in order to worship God. In this

---

[1] If He Only Knew by Gary Smalley, Pg 148

way, the Jewish people "passed on their faith through repetition."[2] Just like looking forward to the traditions that surround Christmas, Thanksgiving, or Independence Day, God provides for us an anticipated way to celebrate through tradition, habit, and repetition.

Now, what I'm not suggesting is that we take up the Jewish festivals and celebrate them ourselves. God has not called the believer in Christ to take on the Jewish faith as well. The entire book of Galatians (and other texts) makes it clear that none of the Jewish traditions are necessary to complete our faith. The scripture declares that Jesus is, "the author and finisher of our faith" (Hebrews 12:2, NKJV). What I am saying is that, together with our children, we should learn from the same lessons the festivals teach and pass these lessons along, so we may lead our children spiritually. These festivals not only teach the tenants of the Jewish faith, but they are fulfilled fully in Christ. Jesus said, "Do not think that I have come to abolish the Law or the Prophets; I have not come to abolish them but to fulfill them." (Matthew 5:17) Therefore we can understand the festivals from a distinctly Christian perspective, passing along foundational truths such as grace, and holiness.

In the pages that follow, we will unpack how to worship God together as a family. We won't leave you hanging to guess how to make disciples in your home. You have the festivals that God put in place to guide you. You can lead your family spiritually. It is rewarding and fun. Start the adventure.

---

[2] The Appointed Times, Jesus in the Feasts of Israel

How Else Will They Know

<u>Family Discussion</u>:

What are the most memorable experiences you have had as a family?

How did it impact you?

<u>Kid's Question</u>:

What is something you've learned by watching a parent, teacher, or guardian?

<u>Parent Portal</u>:

What excites you about leading your family spiritually?

What reservations do you have about leading them?

How Else Will They Know

2 YOU CAN DO THIS

Counter Cultural Kids

The truth is someone is influencing your kids every day. Some of those influences are good – teachers, coaches, school administrators, and even some peers that have high character and are good role models. Yet, even the majority of these good influences are not making a spiritual investment in your kid. They are not leading them astray, but they are not necessarily leading them closer to God either.

Then you have bad influences. I don't think it necessary to list all the ungodly messages that our kids are getting through social media, music, movies, TV, and their peers to name a few. Because of these dangers, it is a common approach for Christian parents to shelter their kids from these things (and I agree with that idea), but no matter how much you try, those negative influences will creep in at the ballfield, at the Christian school, and plenty of others places we deem as "safe". Yes, we limit these pressures as best we can, but we also need to admit that they are still there.

Who is influencing your kid? Better yet, who is influencing your kids for Christ? I bet you can name on one hand the number of people who are taking an interest in your kid's spiritual growth. Set your mind to be one of them. All these other influences can be counteracted, and *no one* is positioned to help your kid grow like you are. You have the best seat in the house! You can be used by God to create a culture in your home that has values which honor Him above the value systems learned elsewhere from other influences.

What Your Kid Needs

Your children need you to influence them. And while you have a full plate between your job, raising a family, their activities, and the slew of other things that occupy your days, you sense that you need to invest in them spiritually. You absolutely do. You will benefit from it, but they *need* it. Your child needs you to take an interest in their spiritual growth. So, as parents, you and I are left with a choice – either we invest in our kids, or we leave it to someone else to do it. Let me challenge you to take this responsibility on yourself. Since you are reading this book, I'm guessing you have something stirring inside you to do just that – to be a major influence for Christ in the life of your children. Thank God for that!

Now, just because you are still reading, it doesn't mean that anything will change. You have an interest, but you also have plenty of reasons you question whether you can do this. You don't know where you will find the time, so you'll need to make the time. It won't be convenient, so you'll have to make sacrifices. You won't always feel like it is making a difference, so you'll have to coach yourself to persevere. There will be moments of victory that make you think you have this parenting thing figured out, and setbacks that leave you questioning your whole approach to parenting. As parents of three teenagers, my wife and I have faced each of these challenges and emotions too. It won't be easy, but it can be done. You can lead your family spiritually! And when you become intentional about helping your kids thrive in their relationship with God, there is absolutely nothing more rewarding. Winning championships, getting ribbons, trophies, awards, certificates, and achievements in academics, sports, and the arts have brought our family joy over the years, but nothing compared to the victories we've seen in the character and convictions of our kids. That is a reward that doesn't just go on the shelf, but one that lasts through this lifetime into eternity.

Seeing Past the Now

It is unlikely that you categorize your life based on what is temporary versus what is eternal, but let's consider those two options. The temporary things in life are pressing, and therefore get most of our

How Else Will They Know

attention and energy. When you cease a temporary activity, the results show up quickly. Just think of not doing any dishes for a week, you'll see what I mean. On the other hand, the eternal things, the things that will matter in God's kingdom 10,000 years from now are far more important, but seemingly less urgent. If we let them slide today, or for a week, we see little to no results for the good or bad. And because we can get away with it for now, we often fail to do the most important things simply because we don't see immediate results.

Wisdom calls for us to look past the immediate pressures of today and this week and take a long-term approach to prioritizing what is most important. Being a spiritual help to your children may not show up on the scoreboard today or next week, but it will likely be evidenced in the years to come. It is the law of sowing and reaping. A farmer plants the seed in the ground, and waters it, fertilizes it, and keeps the pests away. They put in a ton of work, and for a long season, have little or nothing to show for it. But they know the harvest is coming. The law of the harvest means that when we invest in our children now, the results will show up later and produce far greater than we sow into them. Because your children are so important, eternally important, make the decision now to invest in them for Christ.

Engage in Church

If I had to guess, I'd say many of you reading this have thought by now, "I need to get my kids into church more". Let me say I'm a big believer in the local church. I know there are some churches and church leaders that have done damage to people, maybe even you, and for that I am sorry. It doesn't change my belief that the church is the hope of the world. I know that every church has its own issues, never coming close to perfection, but I believe the church is the hope of the world. As a pastor of a local church, I've seen the good, bad, and the ugly of church life. Yet I believe the church is the hope of the world. When the church is healthy and right, there is absolutely nothing like it. Yes, get your kids

How Else Will They Know

in church. Get yourself in a Bible-believing church that teaches and practices the Holy Scriptures. There are incredible benefits to worshiping, praying, and studying the Bible together. There is value in supporting and serving one another that you just can't find on your own, or even in your family.

The church you are looking for must be on point on several key teachings in scripture. First, the church must teach and practice that the Bible is its sole authority. Nothing that a person says must take precedence over "thus saith the Lord". A Bible-believing church will hold God's Word in high honor and seek to obey it at every point. Second, the church has to be firm on the fact that Jesus is the Eternal God who became a man in the flesh. There is no room for error on this one. They cannot teach that Jesus was created, or an angel, or an exalted man. Make sure the church you find is clear on this issue. Finally, the right church will teach that salvation is by faith in Jesus alone. You can't add to what Jesus has already done. He paid for all sin by dying on the cross in our place. He purchased forgiveness for those who believe. He rose from the dead, conquering death and offering eternal life to those who receive Him. We dare not cheapen His sacrifice by trying to add our own works to His finished work.

Let me ask you to examine what you believe about these three teachings. Do you believe the Bible is your sole authority? Do you believe that Jesus is God in the flesh? Do you believe that Jesus is God's only way to salvation? If you said yes to all of these, then I have one further question. Have you received Jesus as the Forgiver of your sins and the Leader of your life? This is the most important question anyone can answer. Because it is so important, we have included a more thorough explanation of this decision in Appendix A. If you have any doubts or questions about where you stand with God, please take the time to explore this resource. It is God's desire that you know Him, that you receive His forgiveness, and you live in His love.

How Else Will They Know

Not Just Church

Yes, by all means get your family in church. Let me encourage you to make it a regular habit. There is power in building a healthy habit. I've belonged to a local gym most of my adult life, and I have developed the habit of being there three or four times a week to take care of my body. I can't tell you exactly which exercises I did there two months ago, but I know that I've benefited this week for the investment that I made then. The same holds true in our spiritual development as it does in our physical development. They both build on each other. If you only visit the gym a couple times a month, you don't see much progress, you get really sore, and you are discouraged from coming back. But when you get into a rhythm of exercise, you make gains in stamina, strength, energy level, speed, weight loss, or whatever it is your goal may be. When you and your family come to church just once in a while, it has limited results as well. The people that see the real gains in character, conviction, holiness, usefulness to God, kindness to others, and a strong faith are the people who make a habit of being in church services, small groups, and serving others. Those are the people who are seeing the character and conduct of Christ formed in them.

My advice to any parent is to get your kids involved in church, not just going to a church service. Worship together. Take them to youth group and children's ministry. Serve together. Become a part of the family that the church was intended to be. I know that this will compete with other agendas in schoolwork, sports, and all the other activities that already have you busy, but you won't regret putting their spiritual development before other things. I also have to say that it will never be perfect. My kids have missed youth group because a big test was the next day, or a coach scheduled a practice, but those instances are rare. Now, before you get the picture that I'm an ogre that makes my kids be at the church every time the doors are open, that is not the case. I simply ask that my kids act like a follower of Jesus. Of course, a Christ follower worships with other believers, prays and studies with others,

How Else Will They Know

and serves those in the body of Christ. That is part of what it means to follow Jesus. Our kids never argue with us about going to church or youth group. They know that decision has already been made. We have taken the approach that Joshua took when he said, "...as for me and my household, we will serve the Lord" (Joshua 24:15). What's even better is that they LIKE going to church. When our church stopped in-person services and went to online services only in the Spring of 2020 during the COVID-19 scare, our kids were vocal about it "not being the same" and "wanting to get back to church."

Often when I tell parents that we don't give our kids a choice about coming to church, they react with the statement, "We don't want to push our kids away from God, so we don't make them go to church." I believe this to be a case of being severely misguided. As parents, we make our kids do things all the time. We make them go to school. We don't give them the choice. If we did, a lot of teachers would be looking for jobs! No, we make them go because we know it is good for them. We set up appointments to go to the doctor, the dentist and other professionals because it is good for them. We make them eat vegetables, brush their teeth, and take showers all because we know the benefits for them. We make them do what is best for themselves physically, educationally, and relationally, so why wouldn't we want the best for their souls by making them go to church? I can tell you that very few families operate this way, and I think it is short-sighted. Unintentionally, we are damaging the spiritual future of our kids and the next generation when we don't lead them. I say emphatically – go to church regularly with your kids!

When a parent makes a decision for the entire family, that is what I am calling "Leading from the Front". It is when you set the pace for everyone else. You lead, they follow in kind. There is a time and place for this style of leadership. God's Word recommends this style of leadership to parents in the command God gives them to "bring them up in the training and instruction of the Lord" (Ephesians 6:4). Joshua

How Else Will They Know

demonstrates this style when he said, "as for me and my house, we will serve the Lord". There isn't any wiggle room in that statement. The leadership here is direct and clear. I lead, and you follow.

At other times, leading your family cannot be so heavy-handed, and you will need to utilize the leadership style I am calling "Leading from the Side". This type of leadership means that you give instruction, assistance, encouragement and challenge, but the decision to comply ultimately rests with the other person.

In both styles of leadership, it starts with you as the parent or guardian. Don't just take them to church. Your job as spiritual leader of your home isn't done by just involving them in church. Your kids need to see it in you, hear it from you, discuss it with you, and get their faith affirmed by you.

Tasha is a mother of five. For Christmas each year our church participates in a gift drive to help needy families in our community. Tasha's family helped out. She asked if any of them wanted to contribute some of their allowance to buy the gifts. It was encouraged, but not required to do so. That's leading from the side. Then when it was time to deliver the gifts, she took her daughters with her so that they could see firsthand how much it meant to the family they had helped. She wanted to teach kindness, servanthood, and generosity to her girls. Having her daughters with her was a teaching opportunity that she deemed invaluable, so she had them go, and in this way, she was leading from the front. This story is a beautiful blend of leading both from the side and from the front.

Involving our families in church is a great step, but don't stop there. Let's put it this way. The church simply doesn't get your kids enough to do the job adequately. If you were to take your kid to church every week for an hour, from birth through high school graduation, that would be less than 1,000 hours the church has available to invest in them spiritually. In comparison, if you only are with your kids for 15

14

minutes a day, let's say in the car or at the dinner table, then you would eclipse the total time the church has with your kid by the time they are in 5th Grade. You will likely have exponentially more time with your kid than a pastor or youth leader will. You are the key to influencing your child spiritually!

It is *YOU* that God has placed in their lives to lead them. Going back to Ephesians 6:4, it is clear that God expects the parent or parents to raise their kids with instruction about God. I believe the fathers should take the lead in this, and the mother should also have a vital part. The Proverbs begins by saying, "Listen, my son, to your father's instruction and do not forsake your mother's teaching." (Proverbs 1:8) Ideally, both parents are involved with the spiritual life of their child, but that isn't always the case. If you are a single parent, take on the role of spiritual leader of the home. If you are a grandparent raising kids, take the responsibility. If you have a husband that refuses to lead in this way, take up the mantle, mom. Your kids are counting on you to lead them, though they will never say those words.

Feeling Inadequate

If you've bought into the idea that you are the one responsible for raising your kids in the faith, then you may feel inadequate. I'm a pastor, I've been to seminary, I've been in countless Bible studies and I still feel that way! It can seem overwhelming. That's why I've written this book. I want this to be a resource for well-intended parents that gives them practical help to honor God in their home.

Aside from not having a seminary degree, or not knowing everything you want to know about the Bible, I think the biggest reason this feels intimidating to many is that they didn't have someone who personally helped them grow in their faith. I count it one of the greatest gifts of God that He sent several men into my life to "disciple" me over the years. I realize most people don't have that opportunity. If that is you, don't be discouraged. You can start the cycle, a chain reaction that ripples through generations of people who invest their lives in others spiritually. You just have a learning curve. You can't simply model what someone else has done for you, you'll have to learn through trial and error.

Some feel inadequate because they are at the front end of spiritual growth themselves. But let me reassure you that you don't have to know everything in order to get started. As you are learning and growing with God, you can share what you've learned with your family. You only have to be one step ahead in order to lead.

Brian was a believer, but had limited knowledge of the scriptures. He wanted to grow and influence others, however. In an effort to overcome procrastination, his study took him to the book of Ecclesiastes. He had never read it before, but quickly realized that this book had plenty to say on the subject. As he studied, he shared what he was learning with one of his daughters. She told him that she had recently seen a "Ted Talk" on the subject of procrastination herself. And just like that, Brian was leading his daughter spiritually despite the lack of Bible background he possessed.

If building a stronger base for yourself is important to you, then let me recommend the a few resources for spiritual growth by Impact Discipleship Ministries. They have produced a series of Bible study books that are a great tool to grow in your faith and broaden your understanding of God's Word and His will for your life. You can find these resources at https://impactdisciples.com/ as well as more information regarding this curriculum in Appendix B. Regardless of how incapable you think you are of leading, by God's grace you can successfully lead your family spiritually.

How Else Will They Know

Take Two

Maybe this isn't your first rodeo. You've tried to lead your family spiritually before, but it didn't work out for whatever reason. That is a very real frustration that many Christian parents feel. They feel like they have dropped the ball. What started out with good intentions fizzled under the demands of your daily lives. Some feel like they don't get the support from their spouse, so they stopped, thinking it wasn't worth the tension, awkward conversations, or even arguments. Others feel like they gave it a good try, only to be met with apathy or resistance from their children. Every one of us has an unseen enemy that doesn't want us to succeed in this endeavor, so we are met with resistance at every turn. Whatever your frustration may have been, I've got great news – you'll get frustrated again! It will be hard to start or restart a habit in your family. It always is. Don't let that stop you. Don't be defeated before you begin.

For all the frustration that is sure to come, there will also be fruit. We don't get to control the outcome of our kids' lives, or if they will come to faith, or if they will be missionaries someday, but we CAN create an environment where those things or other blessings of God can come to pass. We can create a culture in our homes where Christ is honored, loved, and obeyed.

Like you, I want to send my kids out into this world from THAT kind of environment. I don't want to send them into adulthood without the knowledge of God, a growing relationship with Jesus, a foundational understanding of the Scriptures, a keen understanding of their purpose in life, or without a love for God and His church. That foundation is the best gift you can give your kids – to love them enough to present the love of God to them over and over again until they genuinely believe it for themselves.

How Else Will They Know

Not Just What, but How

Church leaders are great at telling you what God wants you to do. We have volumes of sermons and Bible studies crafted to tell you what God requires of you. We have far fewer resources that show you how to do something. That's our bad. Look at what God says the purposes are for giving the scriptures to you and I.

> *All Scripture is God-breathed and is useful for teaching, rebuking, correcting and training in righteousness.*
> *2 Timothy 3:16*

Teaching and rebuking - those are "what" kinds of instructions. Correcting and training – those are "how" instructions. God gave us His Word to tell us what He wants (teaching), what He doesn't want (rebuking), how to do it (training), and how not to do something (correcting). We need just as much input in the "how" department as we need in the "what" department.

Now that I've spent two chapters of this book describing what God wants for you and your kids, the rest of this resource is dedicated to how to make that happen. Please understand that I do not intend on giving you a formula, but guiding principles. I've never found that God honors formulas. He didn't approach every person in the Old Testament the same way, and He doesn't work in all our lives exactly the same way. God does use His Word, His Spirit, and His people to impact others. This book will give you tools to be one of those people that God uses in conjunction with the work of His Spirit and the power of His Word to make an eternal difference.

Breaking the Mold

We also recognize that no family is the same, and that each child is a unique one-of-a-kind creation of God. We want all of our kids to have character. But the approach you take in leading one of your kids may be

How Else Will They Know

far less effective with another. What this resource intends to help you do is not to produce cookie cutter Christians out of your children, but to unlock a uniquely beautiful relationship between your kids and their Heavenly Father.

Tailor the discipleship process as much as you can to the individual child. The more you discern what makes them tick, what their dreams are, what they fear the most, and who they are as a person, the better you will be able to adapt a plan to fit them.

Break the mold, throw away the cookie cutter and jump in. You can see your kid or grandkid be a kind, caring person. You can influence them to live with the grace of the Gospel as the centerpiece of their lives. May God grant us all the grace to be an instrument to lead our families in a vibrant faith in Jesus!

How Else Will They Know

Family Discussion:

- How would you rate your family's involvement in church on a scale of one to ten? Why do you give it that rating?
- How can we have better spiritual habits as a family?

Kid's Question:

Finish the following statements:

- When I think of God, I think of ...
- When I think of church, I think of ...

Parent Portal:

- How are you doing at leading yourself? Are you making an intentional effort in your spiritual growth?
- Are you a follower of Christ? If you want clarification on what that means, take a look at Appendix A.

How Else Will They Know

3 THE SABBATH

"Remember the Sabbath day by keeping it holy. Six days you shall labor and do all your work, but the seventh day is a Sabbath to the LORD your God. On it you shall not do any work, neither you, nor your son or daughter, nor your manservant or maidservant, nor your animals, nor the alien within your gates. For in six days the LORD made the heavens and the earth, the sea, and all that is in them, but he rested on the seventh day.

> *Therefore the LORD blessed the Sabbath day and made it holy."*
> *Exodus 20:8-11*

God is giving us a day off. Who doesn't love a day off, right? Still, the concept of having a Sabbath day each week is not a popular one these days. Keeping a Sabbath day in our weekly schedule is not practiced by most Christians. Sure, we are supposed to go to church, and some do out of habit or duty, but that sediment is waning. In fact, according to a survey done in 2018, only 10% of church members attend a worship service four times a month.[3] Clearly participation in weekly worship services has moved past the "legalistic" approach of attending because "that's what you do" to one based more on convenience.

To be clear, the waning popularity of the Sabbath is not due to theological reasons. We see the concept displayed by God in the creation account, as He rested on the seventh day. God did not require rest (see Isaiah 40:28), but modeled it for us. We see it taught explicitly in Exodus, including being a part of the Ten Commandments. It gets reinforced in multiple books of the Old Testament, for a total of 91 references. The Sabbath was a big deal, a required practice of the Jewish people. This was a part of their law. It is not a law like how we

---

[3] Leonard Sweet, Charles Wesley Distinguished Professor of Doctor of Theology Studies at Evangelical Seminary

How Else Will They Know

obey speed limits, meaning something we *should* do, but we're okay as long as we don't get caught, or circumstances necessitate breaking it. It is a law like paying your taxes. You do it or else. You do it regularly and faithfully. The Jewish people took it seriously. So does God. And according to God, so should we.

> *"If you keep your feet from breaking the Sabbath and from doing as you please on my holy day, if you call the Sabbath a delight and the LORD's holy day honorable, and if you honor it by not going your own way and not doing as you please or speaking idle words, then you will find your joy in the LORD, and I will cause you to ride on the heights of the land and to feast on the inheritance of your father Jacob." The mouth of the LORD has spoken.* Isaiah 58:13-14

The New Testament continues to affirm the validity of the Sabbath. It is mentioned 56 times. Though Jesus frequently had issues with how some practiced the Sabbath, He affirmed its importance and practice.

> *Then he said to them, "The Sabbath was made for man, not man for the Sabbath. So the Son of Man is Lord even of the Sabbath."* Mark 2:27-28

Jesus is affirming the practice of observing the Sabbath as something that is beneficial to us. Because God modeled it, the scriptures command it, and Jesus affirmed it, the Sabbath is something that we should practice. It's not a Jewish thing, it is a God thing. God Himself rested on the seventh day. God commanded it for us. He has communicated that message multiple times. Jesus practiced the Sabbath. He taught its merits to His followers. The early church practiced it, both Jewish and Gentile alike. Yes, the Sabbath is a practice that is to be a weekly part of our lives and something that we lead our families to participate in. It is an awesome tool God has given us parents to lead our families and reinforce some foundational lessons for us and our children

What do we do on the Sabbath?

First, to observe the Sabbath, we don't work on that day. This is a major distinction that makes this day different from others. In the Theocracy of Israel, God was the king for the Jewish nation. No other country has ever had this arrangement. As such, the rules for Israel were unique - and it is a good thing they were. The punishment for those who worked on this day was the penalty of death (Exodus 31:15). While this punishment no longer applies today, the principle of not working remains. God has given us six days for us to work, but He gave us this day as a day of rest. I know many who find this difficult to do. There are those whose job requires them to work six or even seven days a week. Others work five, but then end up doing housework, yard work and a host of other chores on this "day of rest". Those who work seven days a week are commended as hard workers, may even get promoted in their company, but they are wearing themselves thin emotionally, physically, relationally, and spiritually as they do so. The medical world has frequently found the benefits of taking a day of rest each week. One such study claimed that a day of reset had the benefit of "increased focus and productivity at work as well as helping with health, memory and creativity."[4] A weekly rest day is prescribed by God as a time to recharge mind, body, and spirit for our good and for our health.

Secondly, the Sabbath is a day to worship corporately with God's people. The Scriptures are clear that this is a time to assemble together in worship of God. The passages that teach us about the Sabbath call it "a day of sacred assembly", a "Sabbath to the Lord", and the "Lord's holy day". Clearly all of these passages teach us that more than the benefits that we get from a day of rest, the purpose of the day itself is

---

[4] 2008 Research study by the University of Illinois

How Else Will They Know

to worship and honor God. God's desire is that we take extra time to focus on Him and to worship him with other believers. Just like we commemorate the sacrifices of veterans on Veterans Day or celebrate people on their birthday, the Sabbath is a day set aside and dedicated to our God. We remember who He is. We celebrate what He has done for us. We make Him the focus of our lives every seven days.

As a pastor, I've heard every reason there is as to why people have missed church. Some reasons are legitimate for sure, but more often it's something that makes me sad (and sometimes I get a laugh) for why people miss church. The reason I've heard that bothers me the most is when people tell me they had a "family day" or "day of rest", as if what they did by NOT coming to church is what God wanted for them and their family. This is a clear indicator that they don't understand the primary reason for the Sabbath. It is not for them. It is for God. The Sabbath isn't a "free day", but a "He day".

Still others say that they will not be at church, but instead will worship God "from home", "at the ball field", or "in the deer stand". They tell me, "You don't have to go to church to be a Christian". Like I said, most of the reasons I hear for missing church grieve me. There are innumerable examples from Scripture and history of the merits of being a vital part of the local church, and worshiping together. In addition to that, it's commanded for us in the New Testament.

> *And let us not neglect our meeting together, as some people do, but encourage one another, especially now that the day of his return is drawing near. Hebrews 10:25*

A growing disciple of Jesus makes being active in corporate worship a priority. There is no getting around that. I know that for some, your work gets in the way, due to an irregular work schedule, or you are required to work on Sunday, so it isn't your Sabbath. First of all, thank you for providing a service for others on this special day. Over the years, I have had plenty of people in the church I pastor work as public servants, work night shifts, work retail, or take extra work as a single parent. All of these are commendable. So again, thank you for what you do. That being said, may I encourage you to fight for Sundays off (or another day if your church provides other service times). You need the church and the church needs you. Be such a great employee that when you request Sunday off, your supervisor goes to bat for you. Do everything in your power to guard this day for its intended purpose.

One man in my church, Ryan, has served in a variety of roles over the years. Early on, he told me, "If you ever need something, just let me know!" So, he has served in children's ministry, student ministry, our small group ministry, and as an elder (among others). He has since teased me that, "when I said I would help, I meant I would take out the trash!" One of the things that has impressed me the most about this servant of God is that he has sacrificed financially to be at corporate worship gatherings and ministry meetings. See, Ryan works as a public servant and relies on extra shifts to provide for his family. Yet, the three years he served as an elder, he took vacation time to be off on Sundays and gave up overtime shifts so that he could be there to shepherd and lead God's people. Now that has to make God smile. That is a great commitment to observing the Sabbath!

What has changed?

Over thousands of years of celebrating the Sabbath, what has changed? The short answer is, "not much." In fact, the only thing about the Sabbath that has changed in most faith traditions is the day of the week that it is celebrated. The seventh day of the week, Saturday, is still the Sabbath day for the Jewish people. And while the Seventh Day Adventist denomination has made a core distinction of continuing to gather on the seventh day, for most Christians, the practice of the Sabbath has moved to Sundays. The Scripture is helpful to understand that shift.

How Else Will They Know

On the first day of the week we came together to break bread.
Paul spoke to the people and, because he intended to leave the
next day, kept on talking until midnight. Acts 20:7

The early church gathered together, took communion, and Paul
preached on the first day of the week, Sunday. All those activities
sound awfully familiar to us church goers. The early church had
switched days for corporate worship and the practice of the Sabbath to
the first day of the week because Jesus was resurrected on Sunday. We
celebrate on Sunday because our ultimate victory came on Sunday. The
defining moment of our faith - that Jesus rose from the dead,
conquering hell, death, and sin in one blow - is the focus of our worship,
so ever since, the vast majority of the followers of Jesus have
worshipped on Sunday

Lessons from Observing the Sabbath

The Sabbath is not something that restricts you, but something that
frees you. By slowing down and worshipping God, we are able to
remember what's most important in life. When done well, it's a day
that makes sense of all our other days. When we observe a Sabbath, it
teaches us and our kids specific, life-changing lessons. So, when you are
"leading from the front" by taking your family to weekly worship, you
will teach your children these valuable lessons of the faith.

#1: God is the Priority

When worship of God at church on Sunday comes before EVERYTHING
else, it settles the issue of priority quite powerfully. It is a lesson that
your children will never forget. While many people say that God is the
priority of their lives, their actions often don't demonstrate that by
keeping His day the way God intended.

If we had an appointment with a famous actress, singer, or politician we
adored, we would make sure that nothing got in the way of being there.

How Else Will They Know

That's the kind of determination and commitment that we can and should demonstrate when it comes to keeping our weekly appointment with God and His people.

Over the years, my wife and I have had to be the "bad guys" many times in order to keep the Sabbath a priority in our home. Our kids have been active in sports and the arts and have been asked to be at events or games on Sundays. Long before that weekend came, we had decided what would take the priority. We would pull aside a new coach on the first night of practice and explain to them our commitment to be in corporate worship on Sundays. We told them that we would miss games because of it. We told them that if that keeps our kid from playing on the team, we would understand, but we wanted them to know upfront our stance. Every coach we've encountered has graciously kept our kid on their team and tried to work around our schedule.

We've had kids spend the night at our house on Saturdays, and our kids have been at other people's houses for a sleepover too many times to count, and every time, we make arrangements to be in worship together. I'm sure this has been an inconvenience to some other parents, and that my kids have missed out on some fun they could have had on Sundays with their friends, but the lesson that is learned is priceless. Our kids believe that corporate worship is important. This is a lesson both my wife and I learned from our parents as well. We went to church on Sundays. It became a priority for us because it was a demonstrated priority for them. We haven't had to lead a Bible study on the Sabbath with our kids. Our actions are enough. We don't have to argue with them about going. THEY have the same convictions we do. If you are a follower of Jesus, you worship Him with others on His day. Also, we've seen the benefit of taking dozens of children to church with us over the years, and by God's grace, several of them have placed their faith in Christ and followed Him in baptism. It is hard to put into words what that does for your child - to see their friend come to faith in

How Else Will They Know

Jesus, knowing that God has used their influence with their friends to change their lives for eternity!

#2: God is to be Obeyed

Saying that Jesus is Lord is easy. It's far more difficult to live like He is Lord. The cliche that "talk is cheap" rings true in many things in life, but none more so when it comes to our devotion to God. What we say with our mouths can be half-hearted, faked, or routine. What we say with our actions is usually genuine. Let's be honest, none of us obey God like we desire to or intend to. We all fall short of God's glory. Yet, there is something real about those who don't use that as an excuse and continue to strive for obedience.

That striving for obedience in practicing the Sabbath is really important. It is a lesson that is louder than anything you say about obedience. Every day my heart goes into rebellion and wants to do its own thing. Every day, I need to be reminded of who God is and what He has done for me. I need the good news preached to me in my daily quiet time with God to settle the issue of who I will obey that day. Observing the Sabbath carries the same weight. It is a weekly reminder of who calls the shots. It's not my day, it's His day. And consequently, it's not my life, it's His life. So, we obey God's command to worship Him on the Sabbath out of obedience. It lays the foundation to answer such questions as, "Why do we pray? Why should I serve? Do I really need to give a tithe or offering? God can't expect me to share my faith, or love my neighbor?" It all comes back to the same answer. It's not because we always feel like it, or because it will be easy, but because God has said so. When we realize that our life is not our own, but one that has been bought by the expensive blood of Christ, then we have all the motivation for obedience we need.

I think the Sabbath is an easy one to obey. All God is asking is that we show up to worship Him with other like-minded people, giving Him the attention, affection, and honor, He deserves, and then to rest. It is so easy, in fact, that I think kids notice when we don't obey it. They must be thinking, "If I don't have to do what God says in this small thing, then what other small things (or big things) can I choose not to obey God in?" Conversely, when you make the worship of God a weekly priority, it communicates loud and clear that God's commands are important, good for us, and critical for us to follow.

#3: God is in Control

While other people are hustling, buying, selling, working, and trying to "get ahead", believers in Jesus are to be resting on Sunday. In a competitive world, how can we justify not jumping in to keep up with everyone else? It is based on the belief that God is in control. Practicing the Sabbath is an act of faith, believing that God can do more within six days than we can do on our own in seven. The question you and I have to answer is if we really believe that. If you struggle to accept that truth, ask God for faith. Read God's word and look to the example of those who went before us and trusted God enough to do things God's way, and reaped the benefits from it. Also, recognize that there are consequences if we don't follow the Sabbath.

> *You have despised my holy things and desecrated my Sabbaths ... they do not distinguish between the holy and the common; they teach that there is no difference between the unclean and the clean; and they shut their eyes to the keeping of my Sabbaths, so that I am profaned among them ...So I will pour out my wrath on them and consume them with my fiery anger, bringing down on their own heads all they have done, declares the Sovereign Lord."* Ezekiel 22:8,26,31

Ezekiel blames the defeat of the nation of Judah by Babylon in part on the Israelites' failure to keep the Sabbath. That's harsh, but it comes from God's Word. It is our responsibility as parents to lead our families to honor God in weekly worship. It's at this point some parents say, "I don't want to force it down their throats, and turn them away from the

How Else Will They Know

faith". While it is possible to go overboard with demanding too much from your kids, deciding that your family will be in worship to honor the Sabbath is not being demanding. It is leading. Regardless of how you lead them, you can't make them believe. That's on them. But parents will be held accountable for leading their children to at least participate, to hear the gospel, to connect with other believers, and give them every opportunity to follow Christ. Joshua led in this way. His words are a great affirmation that we can lead this way too!

> But if serving the Lord seems undesirable to you, then choose for yourselves this day whom you will serve, whether the gods your ancestors served beyond the Euphrates, or the gods of the Amorites, in whose land you are living. **But as for me and my household, we will serve the Lord."** Joshua 24:15 (Bold added)

As the leader of his family, Joshua spoke for his family. Let me encourage you to make a similar decision to lead your family to practice the Sabbath. It is as easy as making the decision and then sticking with it even when it is hard. That's leadership. It's what your kids need. They won't tell you this, but they are looking for you to set the example and lead them spiritually.

If you are already a part of a church, commit to worship weekly. This may have consequences if you obey, but there will be greater consequences later if you don't. If your family is not used to being a part of a corporate worship experience, call a family meeting. Have the meeting over a bowl of ice cream if that helps. Then tell them that you take responsibility for them not following the Sabbath, and you are changing that. Let them know it is because you love them and want the best for them. Tell them what God has convinced you of during this reading. Then, that next Sunday, take your family to church and start a habit that will reap benefits for eternity.

Making any midstream correction has its challenges. You can expect resistance at first. Your kids are going to be tired, grumpy, or my

How Else Will They Know

personal favorite - whinny. They may even lash out at you for making them do this. Persevere. Keep a great attitude. Keep telling them why you believe this is important. Be optimistic and encouraging to family as you start this new habit. It will take several months for this to feel like the new normal. Be transparent about how the church experience is challenging and growing you. Most of all, demonstrate it to your family. A more godly result in you will be hard to argue with.

A friend of mine had a similar experience with his family. In the middle of a difficult time in life, he rediscovered his spiritual roots, and did a complete one-eighty from not pursuing Christ to passionately pursuing Him. My friend began to attend church faithfully, serve consistently, give generously and became a vital part of his church family. And his kids followed. He encouraged them to start coming, even though they had not darkened a door of a church in years. They started coming to worship services and youth meetings. It was an unbelievable joy to see one of his kids place their faith in Christ, get baptized and have the new life Jesus offered. And we continue to pray for his other kids, that they will have a similar story of faith in Christ.

One last thing. Starting a habit is difficult, and you will likely have a setback. Don't let that deter you. This isn't a New Year's Resolution where you are on the hook until you fall off the wagon and then you are done. No, if you miss a week, don't quit. Right the ship and get there next week. The more consistent you are, the more it is expected and the easier it will be (meaning less arguing, complaining, bargaining, or phantom illnesses).

May you and your family enjoy the Sabbath as God intended!

How Else Will They Know

Family Discussion:

What are some benefits you would experience personally, or we would experience as a family if we were involved with other believers?

Kid's Question:

Do you trust your parents enough to follow their lead even if you disagree or don't understand?

Parent Portal:

What adjustments do you need to make **before** Sunday to make the practice of the Sabbath a priority?

Are you committed enough to lead your family to be active in corporate worship, even if there is push back?

4 THE PASSOVER

"Obey these instructions as a lasting ordinance for you and your descendants. When you enter the land that the Lord will give you as he promised, observe this ceremony. **And when your children ask you, 'What does this ceremony mean to you?' then tell them**, *'It is the Passover sacrifice to the Lord, who passed over the houses of the Israelites in Egypt and spared our homes when he struck down the Egyptians! " Then the people bowed down and worshiped. Exodus 12:24–27 (bold added)*

The Passover festival is the first and perhaps the most recognized of the Jewish festivals to those not a part of the faith. But what exactly is the Passover and how does it relate to us as parents today?

The Passover was rooted in the history of the Israelite people, so we've got to travel back to the book of Genesis and Exodus for an explanation. First, God had chosen a people – starting with Abraham, and through the preceding generations to Joseph. God used Joseph to save his family and many others from the effects of a famine that lasted seven years. During this famine, Joseph's father Jacob (also known as Israel), his eleven brothers, and their families uprooted from the land now called Israel and settled in Egypt. The Israelites flourished there and were highly reproductive. So much so, that the Egyptians got worried that the Israelite population would one day grow large enough to overthrow them. In response, the Egyptians forced the descendants of Jacob into slavery.

Years passed. God's people were still in bondage to Pharaoh. They were being oppressed. I'm sure they doubted many times that they were still God's chosen people. Then, God acted. God raised up a man named Moses to lead his people out of Egypt. Now, if you are Pharaoh, you're not just going to let your entire labor force leave because a man claims a God you don't know tells you to. Like you and I would, Pharaoh resisted. In response, God sends a series of plagues on Egypt to

How Else Will They Know

demonstrate His power, and to force the hand of Pharaoh. God turned the Nile River to blood. He sent frogs, gnats, flies, and locusts to swarm the land. God made it utterly dark for days. It was so dark in fact, that they couldn't even move! Now, by this point God might have gotten my attention and yours, but not Pharaoh. So, as a final act to free his people, God warned the Israelites that he would send a destroying angel in the night to kill the first born son of every household in Egypt. The only way to avoid this was to slay a lamb and spread the blood of the animal on the top and sides of their doorways, so that the destroying angel would see the blood and "pass over" the house without harming anyone.

That is exactly what happened. The people of Israel were spared, while every Egyptian household lost a son that night. I know this act of God sounds extreme, and it is. It was due to extreme circumstances. Because of this plague, Pharaoh let the Jewish people go – all of them, along with their livestock, gold, and other gifts given to them from the Egyptians - just so they would leave and the plagues would stop.

The Passover was a major event in the history of the Jewish people. God instructed them to commemorate this moment in their history by celebrating the Passover festival every year.

Curiosity Piqued

As the Jewish families practiced this festival every year, it certainly would catch the eyes of the children as they did so. In Exodus 12, families were instructed to take a year-old lamb into their homes. That animal would be treated with care. They likely named it. It became a beloved part of the home. Then, on the fourteenth day, they were instructed to kill that lamb and use the blood to cover the doorway, just like in the original Passover. I can imagine the kind of reactions that a father or mother would get as they prepared to kill the animal.

How Else Will They Know

"What are you doing with that knife?"

"What are you going to do to Fluffy?"

"What have you done?"

"Why? Why did you kill him?"

As hard as it would be for a child to watch this all happen, God's plan was for this to be a tool for the parents to teach their children about the deliverance that God granted their ancestors from slavery. That story would be reinforced and repeated every year. As they heard of God's rescue and experienced the reality of a blood sacrifice first-hand, a child couldn't help but see that God was one who would hear their prayers and provide them rescue.

Any teacher will tell you that you really have the upper hand in educating a child when their curiosity is piqued. When they start asking questions, you've got them in a sweet spot. By reenacting the original Passover, this festival was a way for God to show each generation His character, His faithfulness, His love for the Jewish people and stimulate them towards faith.[5]

As the years passed, and the Passover ceremony was transmitted from generation to generation, many other elements became a part of the Passover festival, known as the Seder meal. Songs, scripture, and lyrics were sung, providing a way to involve all people of the family and as a memory tool to learn the story. The meal had four cups that you would drink from at certain moments, with each having a specific meaning.

---

[5] Jamieson, R., Fausset, A. R., & Brown, D. (1997). Commentary Critical and Explanatory on the Whole Bible (Vol. 1, p. 56). Oak Harbor, WA

How Else Will They Know

The third cup, for example, is called the "cup of redemption", symbolizing that God had redeemed his people from slavery and given them freedom to worship Him. Most Biblical commentators accept this cup as the one Jesus used to institute Communion for the church. That third cup of redemption was coupled with a piece of matzah (unleavened) bread that was broken earlier in the Seder, and half of the bread was hidden away until the third cup was consumed. The child would wonder about that hidden bread, and why it was broken in half. That was the bread Jesus likely used to represent his body - a body free of sin (like unleavened bread is free of yeast), that would be broken (physically in torture and on the cross), hidden away (in the tomb), and later brought back (as in Jesus' resurrection). Messianic Jews today celebrate the Jewish Seder with this type of understanding, seeing in Jesus the fulfillment of these Seder elements.

God uses creativity, physical elements, repetition, song, and emotional experiences to captivate a young child during the Passover in order to teach them about who He is, and how He works to redeem His people.

What is the point?

So, what is the point of the Jewish Passover? What would a Jewish boy or girl learn about God and their faith from it?

Rescuing God

First of all, they would see God as a rescuing God. They would know the story of a people, their people, stuck in bondage to slavery. In that misery, they would learn that God heard their cries for help. He is the God who hears. He is love. God loves His people. He is the God who acts. He is the God who set them free. God describes Himself in this way:

How Else Will They Know

The LORD said, "I have indeed seen the misery of my people in Egypt. I have heard them crying out because of their slave drivers, and I am concerned about their suffering. So I have come down to rescue them from the hand of the Egyptians and to bring them up out of that land into a good and spacious land..." Exodus 3:7–8

The Passover demonstrates God's willingness to deliver his people. It shines light on His power to provide deliverance. Children would learn that they could not rescue themselves, but that they would rightfully need to depend on God for rescue and help, not just at Passover, but in every part of their lives.

Holy God

Next, they would learn that God is holy. The shedding of blood was a vivid reminder that God doesn't ignore sin, but that a sacrifice was necessary to satisfy God's wrath. That little lamb that a child would have had affection for would have to be slaughtered. That alone shows the weight and gravity of sin. It is a warning of the destructiveness of sin, of a hard heart, and of an unwillingness to obey God. The Exodus account displays the justice of God. God's holy nature demands a payment for sin. There would be no exceptions.

Jesus' Substitution

Finally, they would learn about substitution. Instead of the first born son being killed during the first Passover, a lamb was killed on their behalf. That is a powerful precursor to the sacrificial system that God was about to institute after the Israelites left Egypt in the book of Leviticus. All the sacrifices listed in Leviticus are substitutional in nature. In a substitutional sacrifice, the condemnation that the person presenting the offering deserved is transferred to the animal that was being offered and it would be sacrificed in the guilty person's place. A lamb, bull, dove, or other items would be offered up in payment for the sins of God's people.

Even more powerfully, the Passover is a symbol of the substitutional death that Jesus provides on our behalf. John the Baptist described Jesus as, "the Lamb of God, who takes away the sin of the world!" (John 1:29). Jesus, the perfect and final sacrifice, was coming to once and for all remove the penalty of sin for all who place their faith in his substitutional death for them. Jesus is unique in that He is the only human that had no sin. Since Jesus had no sin Himself, He could offer Himself as the sacrifice to pay for our sin.

> *For Christ also suffered once for sins, the righteous for the unrighteous, to bring you to God. 1 Peter 3:18*

The righteous One, Jesus paid the death penalty for the unrighteous (that's us). He died in our place just like the lamb in the original Passover died in place of the first-born son.

Applying the Principles Today

Our children need to hear and understand the story of the Passover and others like it from God's Word. They need to know that God is still a rescuing God. Thankfully, at that Jewish Seder, Communion was introduced by Jesus as a lasting ordinance. That act of worship is meaningful on many levels, but certainly as a way to remember Jesus' sacrifice, to give thanks for his forgiveness, and to pass along the story of God delivering us from our bondage to sin.

As believers, we have the privilege of participating in communion with our church family (in a worship service or small group), with our earthly families, and when appropriate, have our kids watch us do so. Regardless of who you take communion with, we must be careful to follow God's instructions. First, understand that communion is only for believers. Those who have placed their faith in Christ as their Savior

How Else Will They Know

may take communion, but those without faith in Jesus must not. Secondly, we must examine ourselves before taking communion. We are to let God's Spirit convict us of any unconfessed sin, that we would confess, repent, and ask for God's leadership anew. Always follow these two steps before participating in "The Lord's Supper". We have provided you further teaching and instruction on leading communion for your family in Appendix C.

As you do, allow your kids to observe you taking communion. Early on, they will not be able to participate themselves (assuming that they are unbelievers). Until they make the decision to follow Christ, your kids will be observers of the Lord's Supper, but not participants. It won't take long for your kids to start asking questions just like the children at Passover.

"Why can't I take communion?"

"Why do we drink the juice and eat the bread?"

"What does this mean?"

"When can I do this?"

All these questions are open doors to tell your kids about how God delivered you through Jesus. You can tell them about sin, and how you were a slave to it (being mindful that too many details may distract from the message or be inappropriate). You can tell them how you were powerless to defeat sin in your life on your own. You get to tell them about Jesus - how His death was the payment that covered you from God's wrath. You get the privilege of explaining Jesus' resurrection, and how His life now lives in you and has led you to freedom. In short, communion is God's way of showing He is still the rescuing God, that His holiness still demanded payment, but through the sacrifice of Jesus, our Passover Lamb, we are set free from sin, hell and death. We get to proclaim the good news of Jesus to unbelievers who may be present, and especially our kids.

How Else Will They Know

We've seen the benefits in our church family of exposing children to communion. We are careful to make sure parents understand their role. They are not to allow their kids to participate if they don't have faith. A couple times a year, our church intentionally participates in corporate communion with the children in services. Then we hear stories. Parents tell us it spurred spiritual conversations in their families and we've seen children come to faith in Jesus, with communion being the catalyst God used to get the conversation started.

The prospect of explaining Communion to your kids may fire you up or it may terrify you. If it is the latter, that's not unusual. It just means you haven't had practice telling your deliverance story to others. And practice is all you need. We recommend that you practice by using - a simple outline:

- Your life before you knew Christ (and what was missing)
- How you came to faith in Christ
- How God has since delivered you from sin, fear or any number of things.

This three-part outline is helpful for most to be able to tell their story of coming to faith in Christ. To learn more about telling your story, I recommend the book, *Becoming a Contagious Christian*. You can also use the template for writing out your own story in Appendix D.

God's plan for us is that our deliverance story is followed up with baptism. Baptism isn't a part of our deliverance story, but a way to proclaim it to others. If you get baptized after your kids are born, make sure that they are present for the big moment. And use that opportunity to explain how God delivered you. If you were baptized

How Else Will They Know

before your kids were around, tell them about it. Show them whatever you can from that day - the certificate, Bible, video, pictures, or t-shirt the church gave you. Talk about how your faith came to be, about your emotions that day, and how that act of baptism has helped you grow closer to God.

At the church I pastor, it is a rare occasion when our preschool and elementary age kids are NOT present to witness a baptism in our church. They usually file in the back, or sit up front, so they can hear the story of deliverance, and see the act of obedience in baptism. God uses this exposure to the Gospel to spark a desire for Him, and it becomes a catalyst for children to enter their own relationship with God. Many times, the parent gets the joy of being a part of the process of leading their children to faith in Christ.

Your children can have the same foundation in their lives. They can know the Rescuing God too. So, expose them to communion. Take communion together at church. Take communion together at home if you feel equipped to do so. If you don't, ask a pastor at your church to teach you how. Talk about the significance of the elements, and how one becomes a follower of Jesus. Tell your kids your deliverance story. When they are older, ask them to prepare and share their own story. Celebrate your baptism or theirs like it is the fourth of July, New Year's Eve, Christmas, and their birthday all rolled into one! God will use these experiences to grow the faith of those you get the privilege to lead.

How Else Will They Know

Have someone tell the Passover story (or read it out loud from Exodus 12) and answer the following questions together:

- Why did God rescue the Israelite people? What did God rescue them from?
- Do we need to be rescued today? What does God rescue us from?

Kid's Question:

Have you ever seen people eat bread and drink juice at church? What did you think of that?

Parent Portal:

Can you articulate your own "deliverance" story? If not, take time to write out your testimony.

How can you best expose your family to communion and to take advantage of that opportunity?

How Else Will They Know

5 THE FESTIVAL OF UNLEAVENED BREAD

> *"Celebrate the Festival of Unleavened Bread, because it was on this very day that I brought your divisions out of Egypt. Celebrate this day as a lasting ordinance for the generations to come. In the first month you are to eat bread made without yeast, from the evening of the fourteenth day until the evening of the twenty-first day. For seven days no yeast is to be found in your houses. And anyone, whether foreigner or native-born, who eats anything with yeast in it must be cut off from the community of Israel. Eat nothing made with yeast. Wherever you live, you must eat unleavened bread." Exodus 12:17–20*

There was another festival declared by the Lord that took place in conjunction with the Passover. It is called the Festival of Unleavened Bread. It starts on the 15th day of Aviv, the first month on the Jewish calendar according to Leviticus 23:6. These seven days that follow the Passover are a remembrance of the manner in which the Israelites left Egypt. It harkened back to the days of hastily leaving captivity, on the road towards freedom. The bread on that day didn't have time to rise with yeast in it, so God directed them to make unleavened bread. This explanation is given in Exodus 12, when the festival is instituted, then again as Moses teaches the people of God 40 years later, preparing them to enter the promised land of God.

> *Do not eat it with bread made with yeast, but for seven days eat unleavened bread, the bread of affliction, because you left Egypt in haste—so that all the days of your life you may remember the time of your departure from Egypt. Deuteronomy 16:3*

In this respect, the festival has a distinctly Jewish meaning. It commemorates their hasty departure from their captors. If this were the solitary meaning of the festival, then this would be a really short chapter, or a completely unnecessary one altogether. Yet, there is a secondary purpose to this festival that has a profound impact on our

43

lives as well as those of our children. As we are about to discover, the absence of yeast in the bread is symbolic of the removal of sin from our lives. To drive this point home, let's first look at how unleavened bread is used in the Old Testament

Unleavened bread in the Sacrifices

We find this curious type of bread as a staple in the sacrificial law of God.

> *The priest is to present all these before the LORD and make the sin offering and the burnt offering. He is to present the basket of unleavened bread and is to sacrifice the ram as a fellowship offering to the LORD, together with its grain offering and drink offering. Numbers 6:16–17*

Specifically, this bread was used for a sin offering. When such a sacrifice was made, it was done with an animal without blemish, signifying the holiness or worthiness of the animal for sacrifice. In a like manner, the bread that is prescribed for the sin offering is unleavened bread, bread without yeast, bread that is worthy to be used. In essence, God is describing yeast as symbolic of sin, and unworthy for a holy sacrifice. Therefore, bread without yeast is a picture of holiness.

In and of itself, this one passage is incomplete, but stay with me. The case for unleavened bread as a symbol of purity and holiness is just getting built. There is further scriptural evidence for understanding the bread and the festival in this light.

Unleavened bread in the "Holy Place"

We find the placement of unleavened bread in the temple of God as directed by God. It is called the "Bread of the Presence" and is described in detail in Exodus and Leviticus. It is significant to know that every description of this bread lacks any mention of the ingredient of yeast. Therefore, the Jews placed unleavened bread before God in his

How Else Will They Know

Holy temple, in the "Holy Place" in obedience to God.

> *This bread is to be set out before the LORD regularly, Sabbath after Sabbath, on behalf of the Israelites, as a lasting covenant. Leviticus 24:8*

Just like with the sin offering, when God is concerned with holiness, the use of unleavened bread is commanded. The Bread of the Presence clearly teaches that to be in God's presence means the absence of sin, or symbolically, yeast.

Jesus Gives Clarity

My favorite explanation concerning the meaning of yeast comes from Jesus himself. He tells his disciples:

> *"Be on your guard against the yeast of the Pharisees, which is hypocrisy." Luke 12:1*

The Son of God succinctly clarifies that yeast has more than a base meaning. There is something more significant going on here. Obviously, Jesus paints yeast in a negative light, likening it to the sinful hypocrisy of the Pharisees. Jesus was pointing out the sin of the Jewish leaders, and he used the term "yeast" to make his point. So, if yeast is a symbol of sin, then conversely unleavened bread, bread without yeast is clearly a symbol of sinlessness and holiness.

Paul Piles On

The church in Corinth had issues, just like every church has issues. But when you read the books of first and second Corinthians, two divinely inspired letters from the Apostle Paul to the church there, you can't help but notice one thing. They had *SERIOUS* issues. It is in chapter five of his first letter to Corinth that Paul dives into the ugliest sin that was prevalent in their church - that they had extremely ungodly behavior, and that they were even bragging about it. If you are unfamiliar with

How Else Will They Know

this passage, you would do well to stop and read it at this point. Knowing the context for the following passage gives weight to its meaning.

> *Your boasting is not good. Don't you know that a little yeast leavens the whole batch of dough? Get rid of the old yeast, so that you may be a new unleavened batch—as you really are. For Christ, our Passover lamb, has been sacrificed. Therefore let us keep the Festival, not with the old bread leavened with malice and wickedness, but with the unleavened bread of sincerity and truth. 1 Corinthians 5:6–8*

Paul is saying the same thing that Jesus did. He is making clear that yeast is a symbol for sin. Once it gets in somewhere, it spreads. A little sin can wreck the church, just like a little yeast can permeate a whole batch of bread. Paul is telling the church to get rid of their sinful practices and complacency towards sin. He is calling them away from sin and to "sincerity and truth".

The Bottom Line

Just one of the above passages might leave us in question as to the meaning of unleavened bread and the festival by that name. Yet, taken all together, it is clear that God is communicating a spiritual lesson to the people of Israel, to their children, and to us and our kids. The bottom line is this: We are to be a holy people. We are to seek purity. We are to remove the yeast from our lives, renouncing sin and our rights to stay in it. We are not to simply rely on grace to cover our daily messes without the desire and practice on our part to actively remove sin from our lives. God wants a pure people. God will do his part in that endeavor, but we have to be willing to do our part.

How Else Will They Know

Progress, not Perfection

Sadly, perfect holiness is impossible on this side of heaven. One day all followers of Christ will be completely without sin. That is one of my favorite thoughts about heaven. As of today, we have to deal with the effects of original sin, a nature inside us that gravitates towards selfish desires, a world full of temptations, and an enemy that loves getting us to fall short of holiness. Under those circumstances, it's easy to just give up, thank God for grace, and to wait for heaven for God to make us new. As convenient as that sounds, it is faulty thinking. Giving up on holiness results in ungodly living.

> *Therefore, since we have these promises, dear friends, let us purify ourselves from everything that contaminates body and spirit, perfecting holiness out of reverence for God.*
> *2 Corinthians 7:1*

God's plan is to make us more like him right now, not just some day in heaven. We are told to "perfect holiness" - to keep striving for it, even though we know perfection is unattainable. All of us know what it feels like to struggle with sin, often the same sin over and over again, and feel defeated. It is not an issue of perfection, but of progress. God is not expecting us to live in holy perfection. God is expecting us to live pursuing holiness. He expects us to make progress in the here and now. Today and the rest of our lives, you and I can grow in holiness.

Lead by Example

This lesson may be the toughest one to teach to your kids, because it requires you to pursue holiness in your own lives. You must be careful to avoid the "yeast of the Pharisees" by acting like you have your act together. You don't. I don't either. And yet at the same time, you need to be growing in holiness, and setting the example. If that sounds like an uncomfortable place to be - striving to be something you can never fully be, but seeking it nevertheless - then you understand how hard this

How Else Will They Know

really is. Let's be honest. No one wants to lead from a place of incompleteness, but that is exactly what God has called you to do, because that is your only choice.

I take that back. You and I do have choices. We can choose to not try. We can give up on trying to be holy ourselves or to lead our kids in it either. I hope you see the futility of that approach. That simply can't be God's path for your life or theirs.

The good news of the Gospel of Jesus is that God has declared us holy through the sacrifice of Jesus.

> *And by that will, we have been made holy through the sacrifice of the body of Jesus Christ once for all.   Hebrews 10:10*

Because of what Jesus did, we are now righteous in God's sight. Our identity has been changed. God sees us as holy. That is how complete the sacrifice of Jesus is for you and I. But God doesn't stop there. He isn't content with us being declared holy; he desires for us to know the joy of living holy. That is what the scriptures are chock full of - encouragement, challenge, and help to live holy with the help of God's Spirit.

Another choice you have is to *ACT* like you've got it all together, by ignoring or glossing over your sin, while picking out the sin in your kids' lives. That's a classic blunder. It's also human nature. It is what the Pharisees did. It's what we'll try to do if we're not careful.

> *I have a message from God in my heart concerning the sinfulness of the wicked:*
>
> *There is no fear of God before their eyes.*
>
> *In their own eyes they flatter themselves too much to detect or hate their sin   Psalm 36:1–2*

48

How Else Will They Know

Jesus tackled this issue in Matthew chapter seven. He likened this tendency to gloss over our sin to trying to get a tiny speck out of someone else's eyes while you ignore the 2x4 in your own eye. You and I can't correct things we can't see. So, we begin by admitting we have areas in our own lives where we fall short. We choose to be honest about those things. We don't hide them. We confess them to God. Then we gladly receive God's grace of forgiveness, and seek His help to overcome them.

If you aren't seeking to grow in holiness, if you can't admit your own sin, if you don't have sincere remorse over sin, you need to put down this book. You lose your right to lead your kids spiritually if you aren't willing to let God have his way in your life. Be willing to admit your own faults.

When you sin against someone in the family, come to them in humility and ask them to forgive you even as you ask God for his forgiveness. I can't tell you how powerful of an example this is. I can't tell you how much intimacy this builds in the family. It's hard to quantify how much trust this builds. It is amazing how much more real grace becomes. I've also been amazed at just how quick my kids have been to forgive me when I do. They are *EAGER* to forgive me when I come as quickly as I can, as humbly as I can, and as sincerely as I can to make things right and own up to my sin.

A third choice is to grow in holiness ourselves, but FAILING to help our kids with the same thing. At this point, let me be clear - I believe this is primarily God's business. He is the One who convicts people of sin. He is the One who holds the standard of perfection. He is the One who gives us the desire for holiness. He is the One who has declared us holy in His eyes. He is the One who can give us victories in pursuing holiness. God is the One who is actively working with your kids for their holiness. That being said, I do believe that parents have a secondary role in helping form the character of our kids

How Else Will They Know

Helping towards Holiness

Ultimately, we lead towards holiness in our families from a place of brokenness because it is our only choice. We are seeking for God to be at work in us at the same time we are to be used by God to help our families.

Like many of the other festivals, God makes it a point of giving the responsibility for leading the child through the practice and meaning of the Feast of Unleavened Bread on the parents.

> *Eat unleavened bread during those seven days; nothing with yeast in it is to be seen among you, nor shall any yeast be seen anywhere within your borders. On that day **tell your son**, 'I do this because of what the LORD did for me when I came out of Egypt.' This observance will be for you like a sign on your hand and a reminder on your forehead that this law of the LORD is to be on your lips. For the LORD brought you out of Egypt with his mighty hand. Exodus 13:7–9*

God is saying, "This is a lesson your kids need to get. Don't let them miss the significance of God's deliverance. Don't let them miss the meaning of removing the yeast from the camp. Sin is destructive and needs to be removed at all costs. Help them internalize God's commands so that they just flow off their tongues and are evidenced in their lives." That is our calling as parents.

Our Action Points:

- Pursue holiness
- Confess our sins to our kids
- Train them in holiness

How to Help

Over the years I have blown it BIG TIME in this area. My desire to help my kids in holiness has come across the wrong way many times.

How Else Will They Know

Sometimes I've corrected them out of frustration. I've disciplined them because I was annoyed. I have questioned their character when really it was me with the issue. I have witnessed many other parents make similar mistakes. I've shared the same regrets with dozens of moms, dads, grandparents, and guardians. So, the following are several guiding principles useful in partnering with God in your child's pursuit of holiness.

Encourage more than you Correct

This is huge. If you are a parent that is always pointing out faults, but never (or rarely) offering praise, you are setting your kids up for an "embittered" spirit (Ephesians 6:4). It's a recipe for your kid feeling like they are "never good enough" for not only you, but for our Heavenly Father. It does more harm than good. Parents, be sure to encourage as much as you correct. You can't do one without the other. A barrage of rebukes will ultimately build a wall up where nothing constructive gets through. Your kids will simply shut you out emotionally, rather than take the abuse. The resulting damage to a child's sense of worth and value is staggering.

For some of us parents, that means we need to adjust our expectations. We can't expect our kids to be little adults. They aren't. They are going to screw up. When our oldest started driving, I told my wife, "Get ready for the phone call where something gets dented." Mistakes are going to be made, and people are going to have bad days, including our kids. We have to be careful to show grace. We are not to point out every fault of our kids. Can you imagine living under that kind of pressure? Focus on the big stuff, namely, their character. Make it a point to not overreact or to hold your tongue when they do something dumb but not dangerous. Ask questions instead of pointing out the obvious. Your kids will learn that you are actually on their side instead of trying to make them into something they are not.

How Else Will They Know

Some of us need to learn a new skill. We are not accustomed to giving a pat on the back or being liberal with our compliments. Instead, we give them out like they are solid gold bars - being stingy with every last one of them. This has been my mentality, and I'm not even sure why. Along the way I realized that I have an endless supply of compliments and encouraging words at my disposal, so I can and should give them away generously.

My wife has the spiritual gift of encouragement, and if that's you, you can be such a blessing to your kids. Use that gift with them. Point out where they please you and instruct them to keep doing things that please the Lord. For the rest of us, we need to learn this skill. What comes naturally for some can become a discipline for the rest of us.

Be Gentle

It's not what you say, it's how you say it. Experts say that only 5 percent of communication is what we actually say. The other 95 percent comes from our body language, our volume, our tone of voice, and how we craft our words. It's not what you say, it's how you say it. You might need to put that one on your dresser to recite over and over. We need to pay attention to our non-verbal cues when we talk with anyone, but especially when we are led to address a personal issue of our child. Some rules of engagement include:

1. Watch your tone of voice

2. Do not yell

3. Do not call names

4. Do not touch them when you are angry

5. Talk to them in person. Technology has its place, but it really has no place in a conversation like this. Our family doesn't have "hard conversations" over text. The tone and intent of the

message is almost always misconstrued and taken more harshly than intended. And while a phone call is better than text or social media, it still leaves a lot to be desired because it is missing all the non-verbal communication. If it's worth correcting, it's worth doing correctly. Go to your child in person and talk it out.

Talk to them privately. Some of my biggest mistakes as a parent have happened in the living room, airing out issues with someone in the family in front of the rest of the family. That is totally unfair. When we make someone's private business public, we instantly put them on the defensive. No one wants to look bad in front of others. When we challenge our kids in front of others, they are going to react badly. They are trying to save face. They want to maintain some sort of dignity, so they dig in their heels and resist us at every point if we do it in public. When I get this right, I ask the person I want to talk to go into the other room to talk with me. This gives them an opportunity to let their guard down. They can be more honest with me, and they are far more willing to admit their faults to just me.

Get on their level

If your kids are little, you can take this statement literally. Physically get down on their level and look them in the eyes. When you don't, you stand as an opposing figure over your kids, especially if you are angry. Getting down on their level like this is a reminder of just how small they are. They are fragile. Treat them as such.

Regardless of their stature, it is important to "get on their level" in terms of understanding. If you are like me, you tend to make assumptions about what has happened, why it happened, and everything in between. The thing is, assumptions are not only dangerous, they don't lead towards understanding. Many times, our assumptions are wrong. So, instead of having assumptions, use questions. Let your kids fill in the blanks, and not your imagination.

How Else Will They Know

When we ask open-ended questions, we give the other person an opportunity to explain themselves. It is amazing what you will learn if you do. Here are a few examples:

"How do you think that went?"

"What did you learn about yourself from this experience?"

"How does that compliment or conflict with your faith?"

"What did you learn about God from this experience?"

This is just a sampling of questions you can use to draw out understanding and teachable moments for your children. For more ideas, we've included a list of "Coaching Questions" in Appendix E that you may find helpful.

For a season in our family, our middle son and youngest daughter fought all the time. We usually learned of it when we would hear our son yell at our daughter from across the house. As we ran to the rescue, it wasn't long until either my wife or I would be getting on to our son. I mean, why did he have to YELL like that? Looking back, it was out of irritation that I came into the picture to make it simply stop. Funny enough, after a while we started to realize that our little toddler princess was actually the instigator of many of these conflicts, and our son was reacting (albeit loudly) out of a response to her being out of line. I believe we would have discerned this far sooner if we had simply stopped to get on his level by asking questions, and listening. So on behalf of mom and me, "Sorry son!"

Attack the Problem, not the Person

This is a powerful distinction. The person isn't the problem. The problem is the problem. So, when we address sin in the lives of others, we have to choose our words wisely to avoid them thinking we are attacking them as a person. If someone thinks they are being attacked,

How Else Will They Know

they bow up. But, if someone believes you are working with them to help them with a problem, they are far more likely to cooperate. Attack the problem.

To attack the problem, not the person, avoid the phrases:

- "You always…"
- "You never…" That puts them in the crosshairs.
- "I'm disappointed in YOU" Rather, say, "I'm disappointed in what you did." Be sure to affirm your love for them even as you point out the problem.
- "You are such a …" I'm saying it again. Never call names. There is no other way to take name calling other than as an attack. Name calling never helps and always hurts. It's one of the most blatant forms of personal attack.

We know we are making progress in this area, when the first emotion we feel in the midst of conflict and correction is no longer anger, but sadness. We should feel bad for our kids when we see that sin is messing with them. We should empathize with their plight and not get angry over how their sin affects us. Making that distinction is helpful to keep the attack set squarely on the problem and not the child that you love.

The Benefits of Holiness

Why do we wallow through the mud of sin with our kids? Because the benefits are amazing! When we get a victory in our lives, we have joy. When we help our kids see, repent from, and overcome the sin in their lives, it results in joy and celebration that is over the top. That's exactly what the scriptures describe for the Festival of Unleavened Bread.

How Else Will They Know

*The Israelites who were present in Jerusalem celebrated the
Festival of Unleavened Bread for seven days with great rejoicing,
while the Levites and priests praised the LORD every day with
resounding instruments dedicated to the LORD.*
2 Chronicles 30:21

When God removes sin from our lives, it is cause for celebration. So,
don't miss this part - celebrate those victories with your kids. When
they speak kindly to their sibling, instead of with apathy, praise them.
When they serve each other, go get ice cream! Holiness is worthy of a
medal, a trophy or any other way you want to make a big deal of God's
purifying work in our lives. Let's have, "great rejoicing". Let's make
some noise about it. Our God is worthy of such praise!

How Else Will They Know

Family Discussion:

What is one behavior that you want to change about yourself?

Kid's Question:

Why does God want us to be good?

Parent Portal:

Give yourself an honest evaluation on how you approach your kids over their behavior. Are you encouraging as well as correcting? Are you gentle? Are you assuming things or asking good questions? Are you attacking the person or the problem? Do you need to ask for forgiveness from anyone you've wronged in these areas?

How Else Will They Know

6 THE FESTIVAL OF FIRST FRUITS

The Lord said to Moses, "Speak to the Israelites and say to them: 'When you enter the land I am going to give you and you reap its harvest, bring to the priest a sheaf of the first grain you harvest. He is to wave the sheaf before the Lord so it will be accepted on your behalf; the priest is to wave it on the day after the Sabbath. Leviticus 23:9-11

The Festival of First Fruits is set during the harvest time in the spring. In ancient Israel, this was a big deal. It was a time of celebration of God's provision for individual families and as a nation. As an agriculturally based society, it's hard to explain just how huge this is. Unless you live on a farm, or grew up farming for a living, you'll likely undersell the significance of this event. The harvest means you and yours would not starve or be destitute. It was during this spring harvest that God instructed his people to bring their "first fruits" of produce before Him.

God had specific instructions on how they were to offer the grains, and other foods before Him. It required animal sacrifice and specific preparations. While those details are significant, it is more helpful to our discussion to focus on the urgency of this offering.

You must not eat any bread, or roasted or new grain, until the very day you bring this offering to your God. Leviticus 23:14

God told the Israelites they couldn't even eat the crops they had harvested until they offered a portion first to Him in worship. That had to get their attention. Could you imagine that today? You and I don't eat until God gets His. Whoa! I can imagine the line at the church building would be a lot like the line at your bank on a Friday afternoon. Everyone would want to do business with God right away. All joking aside, the Festival of First Fruits teaches us (and our children) to view possessions, wealth, work, and provision in light of how God sees them.

How Else Will They Know

It instructs us not only in our practice and handling of these areas of our lives, but also the attitudes that we should have towards them.

God Owns it All

Perhaps the greatest lesson to be learned from this festival is that God owns it all. One Biblical commentator on this passage wrote, "The presentation of the first sheaf was representative of the entire crop, acknowledging that the yield came from the hand of God."[6] First Fruits is an acknowledgement that the harvest came from God. It was a reminder that their daily provision came from God. They were to offer the first of their grain, and what was produced from their animals (like wool from their sheep). It communicates clearly that everything they owned belonged to God, including the land that produced the crop, the crop itself, and their animals.

While the point God is making is clear, accepting it is another story. I'm sure some of the Israelites thought *THEY* had produced the crop. After all, it was by their own sweat that they prepared the soil, planted, and harvested the crop. It was their own hands that fed, and sheared the sheep. It was their hard work that produced the product.

While all that is true, it still doesn't discount the fact that God owns it all. Their hard work would have been for naught if God had not provided the land. Their crop would not have grown if God had not sent the rain. They would not have been able to do any of the above if God had not given them the ability to physically work for it. Their hard work worked in conjunction with God's provision. Yes, they worked, but that doesn't change the fact that it all still belongs to God.

---

[6] Rooker, M. F. (2000). Leviticus (Vol. 3A, p. 286). Nashville: Broadman & Holman Publishers.

How Else Will They Know

Maybe you've had similar thoughts: "I have what I have because I've worked for it." And I would agree with you to a point. God wants us to work hard. Work is a good thing. God gave Adam and Eve work before they sinned. The New Testament also affirms hard work. Paul was inspired by God to write, "If you don't work, you don't eat." (See 2 Thessalonians 3:10). So yes, we work hard. But that doesn't change the fact that it is ultimately God who provides for us.

It is critical to acknowledge that everything you own isn't really yours. It's God's. You've got it on loan. You and I are to manage it well. We are to handle work, money, wealth, and possessions as God instructs us. And believe me, God has a lot to say about these things. There are over 2,350 verses in scripture to guide us in being good managers of God's resources. We would do well to learn God's principles when it comes to saving, giving, debt, spending, etc. God has given us everything we need to know in order to be good managers of His resources. All of these instructions are only helpful if you and I start with and maintain the perspective that it all belongs to God. Check your heart. Is this how you view money? Is this how you are leading your family? As you and I align our thinking and actions to this truth, God can use it to free us from the trappings of worldly thinking and the over-pursuit of riches. It can free us from the dangers of debt. It can give us the joy of giving generously. Financial freedom awaits those who decide that it all belongs to God and that they will handle it according to God's directions.

As a parent or guardian, we model a powerful example to the next generation, either for good or causing harm. The kids in your home will form their views on money largely from you. They will adopt your attitudes. They will model your behavior. They will likely shape their finances according to your teaching (or lack thereof). Since you have this opportunity and responsibility, be sure to teach them. Tell them about the joy you possess when you are obeying God through generous giving. Instruct them to live on less than they make so they can save.

How Else Will They Know

Warn them about the financial bondage that comes with debt. There are plenty of great resources to help you as a parent to dive deeper into this subject. Let me recommend, "Managing Our Finances God's Way". It is a simple, video-driven, God-honoring curriculum that includes practical worksheets and discussion questions. You can purchase this resource on Amazon or by going to shop.crown.org/.

If you have little kids, a curriculum like this is too much. Start teaching them with three jars. Label one jar "Give", one "Save", and one "Spend". Then, when your kids earn money, get an allowance, get birthday money, whatever, teach them how to divide the money among the jars. Show them how to set aside 10% of what they get to "Give" to God. Then take another 10% and put it in the "Save" jar. Put the remaining 80% in the "Spend" jar. This simple practice will go a long way to set the pattern for them for the future and to open up great conversations about why we handle money in this way.

Attitude of Gratitude

Since God owns it all, and he has given us what we need (and often more than we need), the attitude that it is to produce in us is gratitude. God has been kind enough to feed us, clothe us, give us shelter, and provide for our basic needs, and often many of our wants. You ate today. Isn't God good? While some discount praying before a meal as passe, it serves as a powerful reminder of who actually provides for us. It helps us to keep an attitude of gratitude before God. It is something you can do as a family on a daily basis to be reminded that God has once again come through. If not already doing so, the easiest way to practice and pass on an attitude of gratitude is to start giving thanks in prayer as a family. Start with your meals together, but don't stop there. There are all kinds of times to simply acknowledge that it was God who kept you safe, provided for you, has been generous to you, and has been good to you. When we get the spirit of "first fruits" firmly

How Else Will They Know

established in our hearts, we'll see God's provision everywhere and make a point to celebrate God's generosity to us.

> *Every good and perfect gift is from above, coming down from the Father of the heavenly lights, who does not change like shifting shadows. James 1:17*

No doubt about it - everything good in your life comes from God. While that truth is simple, it is not always easy to maintain gratefulness. That's because there is a force that tries to rob us of gratitude. It is called comparison. Comparison robs us of contentment and gratitude. I am happy to drive the car God has provided for me until I see someone else drive by in a shiny sports car. I'm content with my riding lawn mower, until I see the ad for a zero-turn model. I'm ecstatic with the home we live in, until we are driving through a high-end neighborhood. I'm guessing I'm not the only one. Comparison kills contentment. It robs us of gratitude.

This isn't something that only adults struggle with. Your kids are dealing with it too. Through advertisements and peers, they are being sold on the latest and greatest phone, gadget, or gizmo on a regular basis. Both parent and child must work at maintaining gratitude in their hearts. Let me illustrate.

A friend of mine is a high school teacher and coach. While taking his class to the tennis courts, he learned that one of the students had spit on a corvette in the parking lot. Later, the teacher learned which student had done that, so he pulled him aside for a conversation.

He asked, "Why did you do that?"

The student replied, "I don't like rich kids. He doesn't deserve that car."

What the guilty student didn't realize is that the car didn't belong to a student, but was being loaned to them by their grandfather, who had worked most of his life to save for the special car.

How Else Will They Know

Like that misguided student, we make all kinds of assumptions when we compare our lives to others. Comparison breeds resentment, but acceptance breeds contentment. Let's look at what acceptance looks like.

John the Baptist had a huge temptation to live in comparison. He was born right before Jesus, and was his cousin. Talk about being tempted by comparison. Can you imagine what he heard at family get-togethers?

"Your cousin Jesus is such a good boy"

"Did you hear what Jesus did the other day?"

"Why can't you be more like Jesus?"

John could have grown up being compared to the perfect Son of God. Whether he did or not, we really don't know. What we do know is that when they were adults, he absolutely was. John had started a vibrant ministry, calling for people to repent and to get ready for the promised Savior. Large crowds had come to him. Perhaps he had finally grown out of the shadow of his cousin Jesus. Then it happened. Jesus came on the scene. John, knowing now who Jesus really was, baptized him, while feeling so unworthy to do so. Soon after, the followers of John started leaving him and started following Jesus. When the trickle became a flood, some of his most devoted followers came to John and asked him what he was going to do about it. I love what John had to say in response.

> "A person can receive only what is given them from heaven."
> John 3:27

In effect, John was saying, "How many people follow me is up to God." He knew that everything belonged to God, including what his role was in God's plan. It wasn't up to John. It was up to God. That example has helped me let go of so many things that I thought I deserved. I can only

63

receive what God intends to give me. You can only receive what God intends to give you. That's the secret of being content - trusting God to know how much you need, and what you can be trusted with. Can you accept that? Is your heart restless in comparison, or at peace through acceptance? Comparison breeds resentment, but acceptance breeds contentment. I love what pastor Craig Groeschel had to say about this: "Be thankful. Envy is ugly. Envy is resenting God's goodness in other people's lives and ignoring God's goodness in your own life."

Isn't it funny how we compare ourselves to those who have MORE than we do? To keep an attitude of gratitude, wouldn't it make sense to compare ourselves instead to those who are less fortunate than us? I bet you don't do that enough. I don't. If you insist on living in comparison, at least compare what you have accurately. If you want to see how you really stack up, visit http://www.globalrichlist.com/ This site compares what you own and how much you make with everyone else on the planet. Spoiler alert, if you can afford to buy this book, you are way ahead of the curve.

If you want to really drive this point home with your kids, learn about kids in other cultures, and countries. Learn what their daily lives look like. You could also serve as a family at a soup kitchen. Your kids will start to get the picture that they are very privileged. When it comes to being blessed, they will find out quickly that they hit the lottery. This perspective will likely help them to not get trapped in comparison with those who have more. You may want to sponsor a child through a Christian ministry that provides food, clothing, education, and spiritual formation to kids in impoverished places. See Appendix F for recommended ministries that provide such services. All of these ministries will not only give your family a new perspective, they will also provide a name, a story, and a way to personalize this lesson. You'll get pictures, updates, and watch the progress of a child's development. You can pray for them as a family, and send them notes and gifts. You

How Else Will They Know

and your kids will be invested. Your kids may even give up gifts themselves to send special offerings to the children in need.

If you really want to invest in this lesson, a foreign mission trip to an impoverished people group would be life changing. Your kids will never look at their stuff the same. I'm willing to bet they will complain less about what they don't have. One of our family goals is to take all three of our kids on just such a trip. We have two down and one to go. The choice to do these trips will cost us thousands of dollars, but we believe the experience is priceless. We want our kids to have this perspective. We want to go "on mission" with them, and spend a whole week one-on-one with each of them. But if we're honest, the change in perspective is really the greatest benefit of the whole experience. If you have the desire to do the same thing, let me challenge you to not let money keep you from a trip like this. Ask for support from friends and family. Ask your church leadership to chip in. Make it a savings goal as a family. Invest in your kid's heart by leading them on a trip like this. No way you'll be disappointed if they come home with a new perspective of gratitude.

To practice gratitude, give thanks to God as a family. Make it a part of your prayer life. When was the last time you told God you were thankful for what you have? Make a point of specifically listing out the things that you are thankful for. When was the last time you made a list like this? Take advantage of holidays that celebrate this virtue. If you live in the United States, leverage Thanksgiving as a way to talk, pray, make lists, and develop habits of gratitude. For example, a friend of mine started one Thanksgiving by listing three unique things he was thankful for everyday *FOR A YEAR*. When you do the math, that's a list of 1,095 things (people, things, answered prayers, etc.) that he named in thanks to God. May we cultivate gratitude in our hearts and the hearts of our kids in a similar manner.

Attitude of Humility

Not only did the Festival of First Fruits intend to cultivate an attitude of gratitude, it also served to promote an attitude of humility. When God owns it all, you can't brag about what is not yours. When God is the provider, you can't take credit for paying the bills. It isn't your smarts, your skills, your brawn, or anything else you brought to the table that put you in a favorable position. It was God. When God gets the credit for the good things in our lives, that's the practice of humility. Look at how the Festival of First Fruits was detailed for the people of Israel through Moses before they entered the promised land.

> *He brought us to this place and gave us this land, a land flowing with milk and honey; and now I bring the firstfruits of the soil that you, LORD, have given me." Place the basket before the LORD your God and bow down before him.*
> *Deuteronomy 26:9–10*

Moses reminded the people that all this good stuff they were about to receive was God's doing, not theirs. As a symbol of humility, the people were instructed to present the offering of grains from a bowed position before God. They were to humble themselves before God. The whole experience was an expression of the fact that God is in control. It expressed their need for God. It elevates God to where He belongs in our hearts - high above ourselves.

In a world that encourages promoting self, God tells us to promote Him. Practicing humility is the only way to battle against the pride that tries to creep up in our hearts.

Several years ago, I was in a pickle. I had received several letters from our Home Owners Association, instructing me to repaint our house (it certainly needed it). They were threatening to put a lien on the mortgage. And, while they weren't exactly nice about it, I agreed it needed to be done. I was making plans to paint our house myself. Then it happened. I got on a motorcycle. I'll spare you the details (and me the embarrassment), but the short of it was that I fell off the bike, breaking my collar bone, and three of my ribs. I wasn't going to be painting anytime soon. Yet, the letters kept coming. I knew I had no recourse. I didn't have the thousands of dollars that would be needed to hire someone to paint the house. Then, I got the news - the elders at our church had approved paying for our house to be painted - as a gift. I was overwhelmed. I was moved to tears. It was humbling, in such a good way. I was powerless to help myself and they bailed me out. God used them to provide for us. In actuality, that's what God does for us every day. He is the one making a way when there is no way. He is the one providing when we can't provide ourselves. He is the one taking care of us, often while we live in the illusion that we are the one's taking care of business.

You and I owe it to ourselves and to our kids to humbly point to God as the one who is taking care of us. Honestly, do you really think that you've got it all figured out? Me neither. So, why do we give the impression to our kids that we do? When you and I talk honestly about our inability, it opens the door for God's ability. When we brag on God, it will give your kids confidence to move into adulthood, not because they will have it all figured out, but because they are trusting and following the God who does!

Leading from the Side

In chapters One and Two, I described what it means to "lead from the front" in regards to involving your kids in the life of the church. Leading from the front is an authoritative form of leadership. And while I recommend it in certain areas of spiritual development for your kids, I don't recommend it for others. There are times when leadership isn't about authority, but about influence. I call this type of leadership "leading from the side". The best leaders leverage a combination of both types of leadership.

When we try to cultivate attitudes of the heart in our kids, let's face it - we can't force it. Our part is to model gratitude, to give God credit for our jobs, to give thanks to God for paid bills, and for providing what we

How Else Will They Know

need. Our part is to pray, asking God to change our hearts and the hearts of our kids. Our part is to teach the principles, knowing only God can cause it to take root in the lives of others. These are "lead from the side" types of behavior.

I am getting an intense tutorial of "leading from the side" from my kids these days. My kids are all in the early stages of being drivers. Two of them have been driving less than a year with their license and the other has her permit. Pray for me! Why? I'm the one in the passenger seat as they are learning. I can teach, guide, and influence their thinking, but they are the ones that are driving. All I have is influence and the useless air brake on my side of the car! While I love seeing my kids mature and gain freedoms through driving, I am gaining valuable experience of just what it means to lead well from the side.

Your kids and my kids need us to lead them well from the front and the side spiritually. You can't make someone love God. You can't make someone want to grow in their faith. From the side, you can't force any of that, but you can nurture it. You have incredible influence with your kids, even when they don't give any indication that you do. May God use you to lead your kids to live with gratitude, humility, and to handle their resources in a way that pleases our Heavenly Father.

How Else Will They Know

Family Discussion:

How can we consistently acknowledge that God is the One providing for us?

Kid's Question:

Do you struggle with comparing yourself or your stuff with other people?

Parent Portal:

How would you like to cultivate gratitude and humility in your own life?

How can you "lead from the side" to promote gratitude and humility in the hearts of your children?

How Else Will They Know

7 THE FESTIVAL OF WEEKS

> Count off seven weeks from the time you begin to put the sickle to the standing grain. Then celebrate the Festival of Weeks to the Lord your God by giving a freewill offering in proportion to the blessings the Lord your God has given you. And rejoice before the Lord your God at the place he will choose as a dwelling for his Name - you, your sons and daughters, your male & female servants, the Levites in your towns, and the foreigners, the fatherless and the widows living among you. Remember that you were slaves in Egypt, and follow carefully these decrees. Deuteronomy 16:9–12

The Festival of Weeks is described in the scripture above and previously in scripture in the passages of Leviticus 23:15–22 and Numbers 28:26–31. The Festival of Weeks occurs 50 days after the Festival of First Fruits. That is where the term Pentecost later came from (Pentecost is the Greek term for fiftieth). Pentecost and The Festival of Weeks are the same event. It is the last of the Spring Festivals. Where the Festival of First Fruits was an offering celebrating God's faithfulness at the beginning of the Spring harvest, the Festival of Weeks is an offering coming at the end of the season, when the full harvest had come in.

Giving Just Because

The Festival of Weeks is a harvest festival and as such, it clearly teaches that the harvest is from God, and that His people are to give back to Him from what God has provided. This principle was taught in the practice of the Festival of First Fruits, which we previously covered. While the same message is conveyed through this festival, reinforcing the same principles of God's ownership, God's generosity, and God's provision, we will not repeat those same lessons here again. In addition to teaching generosity towards God, the Festival of Weeks has a unique lesson for us and our children.

How Else Will They Know

This offering was a freewill offering. That means that unlike the Day of Atonement (see chapter 9), it was not given because you had sinned. Unlike the Festival of First Fruits, it was given not because you owed a specific amount to God. The sacrifice given at the Festival of Weeks was given because you wanted to give, "just because" you recognized that God is good and that He has been good to you. It acknowledges that God blessed you out of His own goodness, and in response, you love Him for it. The Festival of Weeks teaches us to love God for who He is, and what He has done.

One commentator describes the intent of the festival. "This feast was to be kept with sacrificial gifts according to the measure of the free-will offerings of their hand, i.e., voluntary offerings which they gave as the Lord had blessed them; nothing was specifically prescribed, each was to give of his own free-will as the lord had prospered him."[7]

We have many reasons to feel the same way towards God. God is our creator. He is the Great Provider. He is generous, often giving us more than we need. He shows kindness while being patient with us. He loves us so much that He provides His Son Jesus as the perfect offering for our sin, removing our guilt and making us righteous in His sight by faith. For all these reasons, and so many more, God is worthy of our unsolicited offerings of thanks, praise, obedience and love. When we give God those things, it is a gesture of our love for Him and that is pleasing to Him.

So let's not breeze past this thought. Take some time to think about the attributes or qualities that you love about God. These are not things that God has done, but simply who God is. You might want to focus on

---

[7] Spence-Jones, H. D. M. (Ed.). (1909). Deuteronomy (p. 271). London; New York: Funk & Wagnalls Company.

How Else Will They Know

God's goodness, His power, or His love to name a few. Take some time to write these down and then pray over the list, thanking God for each of these. I've included a list of some of God's attributes in Appendix G for your use.

Now, think about the things God has done for you, for your family, or for humanity. Make a list of specific actions God has done from answered prayers, to arranging circumstances, to how He has provided salvation. Once this list is written, pray over it as well, thanking God for what He has done.

These prayers you just prayed are in essence a "freewill offering" to God. You didn't have to do it, but you did. That is the spirit behind the Festival of Weeks.

Giving to Those in Need

Giving to God "just because" is a beautiful thing, but God never intended for our offerings to stop there. Yes, we offer God our very lives, but a heart of gratitude also offers gifts to others as a way to honor God as well. The harvest time was the perfect time to be generous to not only God, but to those in need. The Festival of Weeks came with some additional instructions to make sure this point wasn't missed by the people of Israel.

> " 'When you reap the harvest of your land, do not reap to the very edges of your field or gather the gleanings of your harvest. Leave them for the poor and for the foreigner residing among you. I am the LORD your God.' " Leviticus 23:22

This festival teaches people to leave a margin of their crops for the poor. The farmer would leave parts of their fields unharvested so that those in need could gather the grain and in doing so, have their needs provided for. It was a practical solution to provide for those in need and a way for everyone to participate.

How Else Will They Know

All the members of the community, regardless of their social or economic status, were invited to participate in the festivities. The most disadvantaged among them were, in fact, especially to be welcomed. God's reference to the "foreigner" was a prompt for Israel to remember how the Lord had freed them from their own bondage in Egypt, and had since given them so many blessings. One commentator writes, "The sign of that divine favor was the produce itself, a portion of which must be presented to the Lord and to his needy people."[8]

Today, very few of us are farmers. Modern technology and hard work allow a few people to provide for the rest of us. So, without fields to allow people to pick grain from, how do we participate in the spirit of this festival? Simple. We give to the poor. We find ways to be a blessing to those in need. We do so because God has been so good to us by allowing us to have more than we need. The New Testament church continued to show the spirit of generosity to those in need. Read Paul's God-inspired instructions to the church in Corinth.

> *Now about the collection for the Lord's people: Do what I told the Galatian churches to do. On the first day of every week, each one of you should set aside a sum of money in keeping with your income, saving it up, so that when I come no collections will have to be made. 1 Corinthians 16:1–2*

Notice who this collection was for - the Lord's people. God wants us to give out of a couple of different pockets. First, He asks us to give a tithe or offering to Him. Here, He asks that we give to others in need. If you are like me, you don't know tons of people in financial need. In reality, they are all around us. We can help them as we intentionally look for ways to be God's instrument in meeting their needs. In addition, when

---

[8] Merrill, E. H. (1994). Deuteronomy (Vol. 4, p. 254). Nashville: Broadman & Holman Publishers.

How Else Will They Know

we involve our children in caring for the poor, they learn this lesson through experience and practice. It is a lesson they won't soon forget.

I was powerfully reminded of the importance of this practice earlier this year. I had unexplainably volunteered to chaperone our church's youth trip to an amusement park. I guess that it proves a sucker is born every minute! While I was glad to go because my entire family was going, to be transparent, I had not had a good day. I got angry at one family showing up late to the church. I had a conflict with one of the youths. I had been grumpy for portions of the day. So, when we decided to stop in downtown Atlanta on the way home to eat, I wasn't the most enthused. We stopped at The Varsity, an iconic greasy spoon restaurant that is famous for chili dogs, greasy onion rings, and people from all walks of life. When we arrived, I was in such a hurry to get it over with, I walked in, leaving everyone else behind in the parking lot. When I came back outside to hurry people along, my worst fears were realized - a homeless man was approaching the group. My first instinct was to go into "protection mode" and harshly dismiss the man. As I went to confront the man, God confronted me. God pushed all that grumpy out of my heart in an instant, and replaced it with compassion for the man.

As I approached him, he politely asked if we had any money since he was hungry. Without thinking of the safety of the group, I quickly offered to buy him dinner. As we walked into "The V" together, the youth group and other chaperones were in tow. As we waited in line, Kevin and I had a great conversation. He was an articulate, kind man. I asked about his faith and he affirmed that he was a follower of Jesus. To my surprise, he wasn't trapped in any addiction. He was just at a low point in life and trying to figure some things out. Every assumption I had held was shattered. It really was a joy to talk with this man. God got me out of my own funk and at the same time let me help someone in need. It really was a God-ordained encounter.

What struck me the most though, was the effect it had on the group. It was such a teachable moment for all the people in our group. It communicated that this is what followers of Christ do - we help people in need. We don't have to be suckers, but we can be generous. Later, I learned that my son had snapped a picture of Kevin and I from behind and posted that picture to his Snapchat account, with the caption: "helping someone out...". Apparently, God had touched my son's heart in a profound way through that encounter as well.

As parents, we have a chance to model, teach and lead our kids to be helpful and generous to people in need. There are so many ways we can do this. We can volunteer as a family at a soup kitchen. We can take gifts to families in need at Christmas. There are really too many possibilities to list. The opportunities are everywhere. The question is whether we will take advantage of these ministries and the random encounters that God places in front of us.

Take a two-pronged approach in serving the least of these. Be open to those spontaneous moments where generosity and service can be modeled, and also be intentional to schedule some times to serve others in the community. I recommend finding a ministry that is doing great work, meeting a legitimate need in the community, and that also is unapologetically Christian, serving people in the name of Jesus. When we do so, there is a profound promise Jesus gives:

> "Then the King will say to those on his right, 'Come, you who are blessed by my Father; take your inheritance, the kingdom prepared for you since the creation of the world. For I was hungry and you gave me something to eat, I was thirsty and you gave me something to drink, I was a stranger and you invited me in, I needed clothes and you clothed me, I was sick and you looked after me, I was in prison and you came to visit me.' ...

> "The King will reply, 'Truly I tell you, whatever you did for one of the least of these brothers and sisters of mine, you did for me.' Matthew 25:34-36;40

How Else Will They Know

Every opportunity to minister to the poor, the lonely, and the needy is an opportunity to serve Christ himself. May we be parents that will model and teach our kids to serve those in need and even Christ himself! Sharing these experiences as a family will leave a lasting impression on your children and go a long way in shaping their character in Christ.

Giving of Your Gift

Commentators recognize that the significance of the Festival of Weeks goes beyond that of simply offering something to God. It is a recognition that God has given to us, so that we could also give to others. Look at a couple commentator's descriptions of the Festival of Weeks:

This feast was to be a time of joy and sharing. Since the LORD had been "generous" with the Israelites they were to be generous with others, especially with the less prosperous members of their society.[9]

It was required of them as a tribute to their Sovereign Lord and owner, under whom they held all they had; and yet because the law did not determine the quantum, but it was left to every man's generosity to bring what he chose, and whatever he brought he must give cheerfully, it is therefore called a free-will offering. It was a grateful acknowledgment of the goodness of God to them in the mercies of these corn-harvests now finished, and therefore must be according as God had blessed them. Where God sows plentifully, he expects to reap accordingly." This description of the festival is powerful to me,

---

[9] Deere, J. S. (1985). Deuteronomy. In J. F. Walvoord & R. B. Zuck (Eds.), The Bible Knowledge Commentary: An Exposition of the Scriptures (Vol. 1, pp. 292–293). Wheaton, IL: Victor Books.

How Else Will They Know

especially that last line. "Where God sows plentifully, he expects to reap accordingly" is a principle that we see multiple times in scripture.

> Remember this: Whoever sows sparingly will also reap sparingly, and whoever sows generously will also reap generously.
> 2 Corinthians 9:6

> ... From everyone who has been given much, much will be demanded; and from the one who has been entrusted with much, much more will be asked. Luke 12:48

> A spiritual gift is given to each of us so we can help each other.
> 1 Corinthians 12:7, NLV

Bear with me as I brag on my kids for a moment. As teenagers, all three of them serve in ministries at our church - one on the production team, one as an usher, and one in the Children's ministry. They have each found their place of service. It is a joy to watch them serve God. To be honest, I get emotional seeing them serve. You think I would be used to it by now. Ten years ago, when they were little, they learned quickly that they could pitch in. They were not only the pastor's kids; they were church planter's kids. We set up and tore down our equipment for church every week for just shy of a decade. They knew how to set up chairs, roll boxes down the hall, make coffee, and how to do just about anything the adults did. They were a huge help. From a young age they learned that they had something valuable to give.

The truth is that every believer has something significant to offer others in the form of their spiritual gift. When you came to faith in Christ, God gave you at least one gift like this, where His ability becomes your ability to help others. It is an area where you are supernaturally good at something. That something is to be shared, given away through your time and talent. I believe this is the greatest underutilized resource in the Kingdom of God - the abilities of God's people that don't get used to their full potential.

That doesn't have to be your story. You can discover, use, grow, and maximize the gift God has given you to help others. That is the lesson learned from the Festival of Weeks and the expectation of God as described in the verses above. Trial and error is a valid way to figure out your gift, but as a way to point you in the right direction, an assessment is a helpful tool.

PLACE

While there are all kinds of assessments out there, I recommend PLACE Ministries as an excellent resource. The PLACE assessment is a tool they have developed to help you find your spiritual gift and right fit in ministry. This assessment covers personality type, spiritual gifts, abilities, passions and life experiences. PLACE Ministries has assessments formatted for adults as well as for students. The online version of both assessments can be found at https://www.placeministries.org/ as well as a wealth of information about the assessment itself. We have included in Appendix H information about downloading their free app, "mySpiritualGifts" to get started on your assessment.

Better yet, if your church does not utilize a strategy to help their people serve based on their gifts and wiring, consider asking your church leaders to investigate being trained in how to use the PLACE assessment and process. This way, you not only will have an assessment, you'll have a way to unpack the results and others in your corner to steer you towards your best fit in ministry. When a church implements this strategy, they will be able to provide Biblical teaching to help you

How Else Will They Know

understand your PLACE, compile a database of assessments for the church family, and to provide coaching so that you understand yourself better. Properly trained, any church can give clear direction in using your gift effectively.

The process is helpful for you and for your older children. If you can help steer them to meaningful service in God's church, doing something they love, you've given your kids a great gift! They will discover purpose in serving Christ by helping others. That lesson is one that can connect them to Christ's church beyond merely attending, but also to connect them by contributing. If your kids have a serving commitment that they love, it can help your children stay engaged in the years to come when so many other young adults fall away from the church. Help your kids to discover this kind of purpose. Engage in serving with them. Help them find their PLACE in God's church. Let them discover the joy that is found in giving of themselves to others. Then they will experience life as Jesus intended:

> *Whoever finds their life will lose it, and whoever loses their life for my sake will find it.   Matthew 10:39*

What a privilege we have as parents to help our children give their life away so that they can find the good life that Jesus offers!

How Else Will They Know

What could we do as a family to help someone in need?

Kid's Question:

How do you like helping others?

Parent Portal:

Are you using the gifts God has given you? Do your children know and use their gifts? What is your action step to move you and your family to serving God and people well?

8 THE FESTIVAL OF TRUMPETS

The Lord said to Moses, "Say to the Israelites: 'On the first day of the seventh month you are to have a day of sabbath rest, a sacred assembly commemorated with trumpet blasts. Do no regular work, but present a food offering to the Lord.' "
Leviticus 23:23–25

I don't know how or when you formed your first views on God, but for me, as a child, it was through the loving care of my parents and in the context of a church experience. And my earliest memories of that church family were all positive, except perhaps in this one area - that God dislikes fun. God was revealed as holy, merciful, and loving, but not fun. I don't know if that was my own warped perception of what was being taught, or if that was really the environment I came up in, but that's the message I took with me. God was to be worshipped, honored, even feared, but he was not to be perceived as fun.

Yet, as I studied the Festival of Trumpets, I realized those early concepts of God misrepresented the true nature of God. This festival calls for a week-long party with God as the honored guest. Now isn't that a shocker? We've been told that "all work and no play" is a poor recipe for life from multiple sources, but rarely is that message communicated from the church. Yet, as we dive into this festival, you'll see that having fun, as a nation, as a group of believers, and as a family is a big deal to God.

Commentators on the text above say that the trumpets sounded thirty successive times, for the dual purpose of announcing the commencement of the new agricultural year, and for preparing the people for the approaching feast. "It is a feast of joyous sounds to awaken a nation's... disposition by means of a festival blowing."[10]

---

[10] Lange

How Else Will They Know

The festival week afforded the celebrants an opportunity to thank God for the provision of the previous season and to dedicate the next year's harvest to Him as well. Festival of Trumpets was celebrated early in the Fall, being the first of three festivals in one month, followed by the Day of Atonement and the Feast of Tabernacles. It was a busy time in the life of a Hebrew - (kind of like the month of May in the United States as we celebrate Mother's Day, graduations, and Memorial Day) - and like us, they looked forward to all the fun that came with it.

So, here's the point. As you lead your family, be sure to lead them towards fun. Don't just lead your family in Bible studies and all the serious stuff. Lead their whole person - body, soul and spirit - by including fun on the agenda. There is nothing more life giving and spirit-freeing than a good belly laugh! There is nothing that will bond you to one another like sharing adventure together. There is nothing that takes the emotional walls down better than getting outside our routine, away from work or school, and sharing an experience with those we love. So, accept this part of the job with gusto. It is cliche, but "a family that plays together, stays together".

Recently our family took a trip to a state park to do some hiking. We walked about 3 miles, and we were still feeling good, so we decided to double back and hit some trails we had skipped on our first pass through. On the way back into the trails, we noticed some dark clouds heading our way. I stopped. We were near our car at that moment, but heading away from it if we continued. I pointed out the clouds to everyone else and poised the obvious question, "Do you want to keep going even if that means getting wet?" The unanimous choice was to forge ahead, whether that be wet or dry. About ten minutes later, it started raining. More descriptively, it poured. The bottom dropped out of those clouds and we were soaked. We slipped, we got muddy, and the path became a small stream. The best part, though, was that we laughed. We had a great time laughing at ourselves, laughing at each other, and just cutting loose. We all knew we had made a memory that

How Else Will They Know

would stay with us for years to come. Score one in the fun column!

If I'm being honest, I need to be reminded of this one. Some of you do as well. My wife is far more fun-loving naturally. She can be a big kid, be silly, and be spontaneous. I'm more rigid. I like my routine and sometimes take myself too seriously. So, whether it comes naturally or you've got to "put it on your calendar", make time for fun together as a family. Your creativity and imagination can be cut loose on this one, so I don't want to limit you by the following recommendations, but I believe it's important to think about how we can have fun. Here are my suggestions.

Take Time to Celebrate

Part of having fun together is recognizing times to celebrate. These can be planned events or spontaneous opportunities that you seize. One such unexpected event came during my oldest daughter's senior year of high school. She called my name from her room, and as she rushed down the stairs, she was looking at her phone, then to her mother and I. She said, "I did it. I got accepted to college!" She showed me the acceptance email and then gave me a big bear hug. If you've had an 18 year old daughter, you know that hugs like that don't come along every day, so I hung on for dear life and savored the moment. We thanked God, we touted her hard work, and we had a moment. I told her this was cause for celebration, and that we were going as a family to get ice cream that night. And sure enough, that evening we all piled in the car, we praised her in front of her siblings, and we all picked out our favorite flavors. Why? Because we just had to celebrate!

Just like the return of the wayward son in the parable famously called "The Prodigal Son" found in Luke 15, the Father found that cause for celebration. He had the choice animals prepared for a meal, and he called for a party to be thrown. This shows the celebratory heart of God. God likes a good party! When the faithful son questioned having a party for someone who had screwed up so badly as the other son, I

How Else Will They Know

love what the Father had to say in response: "But we **had** to celebrate and be glad..." (bolding is mine). There was no stopping it. Our Celebratory God had to share his gladness with others! God also shows his propensity for celebrating in the festivals.

Celebrate their big days

> When you go into battle in your own land against an enemy who is oppressing you, sound a blast on the trumpets. Then you will be remembered by the Lord your God and rescued from your enemies. Also at your times of rejoicing - your appointed festivals and New Moon feasts - you are to sound the trumpets over your burnt offerings and fellowship offerings, and they will be a memorial for you before your God. I am the Lord your God." Numbers 10:9–10

In effect God is saying, "Sound the trumpets! Celebrate your big days. Throw a party in honor of the victories I give you. When I rescue you from your enemies, rejoice."

I think for the most part parents already do a good job of this. We celebrate our children's big days like birthdays, graduations, good grades, academic success, athletic achievements, performances, achievement in the arts, and others. And clearly it is good and right to do so. It means the world to our kids when we show up and when we make a big deal about them. It helps them know that their success means something significant to us. It communicates that they are special. And while it may be difficult to be at everything your child is involved in, when we are present for their big days, we make a major investment in the relationship with them.

I am also learning just how important it is to say something, even something succinct, as a way to honor them on their big day. Having a party is great, but affirming them, in front of the family and their friends is life-giving. Now, you don't want to go overboard, or use flattery, but

How Else Will They Know

you do want to tell them how you feel about them. Giving compliments to someone, especially in front of others, goes a long way to building them up. At a birthday party for instance, I'll tell them just how much joy they have brought our family, how we couldn't imagine our lives without them, and how proud we are of the person they are becoming. I may even sprinkle in a cheesy joke or two as well. I usually finish up by praying and thanking God for my child, and for His undeniable work in their lives. Then, we eat cake!

Celebrate their character

While spotting achievements in the areas mentioned previously are pretty easy, this is an area that can slip past us if we're not careful. So let me encourage you to look for and celebrate the successful moments your kids have in the development of their character. We reward them for a sound mind, their skills, or a strong body, so why not a good loving heart? When was the last time you made a big deal of it when your child did the right thing?

I remember my son telling us how while playing on the school basketball team, he had a victory in character. Some of the players were passing a vape around on the bus on the way to a game and were putting pressure on everyone to do it. My son didn't. He stood by his convictions. When he told us that, our hearts soared. We made a big deal out of that, affirming just how proud we are of his decision and for sticking with his convictions!

Another time, one of our daughters noticed that one of her classmates was discouraged. It became clear that this other girl was being left out by her friend group, and in middle school, that means everything. My daughter sent her an encouraging text message and then changed up her usual routine and ate lunch at school with this girl rather than with her usual group. Now, it is one thing to notice someone is in need, but it's another to act on it. We celebrated the character my daughter showed that day in being a minister of Jesus to that friend of hers. That is success in God's eyes!

Celebrate their spiritual milestones

When God tells his people to, "sound the trumpets over your burnt offerings and fellowship offerings" those are significant spiritual events in their lives. God wants us to celebrate those too. When your kid accepts Christ, the world should stop and you celebrate! Throw a party. Take them for ice cream! Their baptism day is a day of celebration, so make a big deal about it. Invite family and friends to the service and then to a party. Those are life-changing spiritual decisions that we can sound the trumpets over.

And don't stop there. Reinforce their godly behavior. When they have a desire to go to church, when they give to the offering, when they read their Bible on their own, when they invite a friend to church, when they share their faith, and when they serve in the church, these are all worthy of recognition and celebration. If you want to see your kids make those decisions and repeat them throughout their lives, then celebrate them. There is an undeniable truth of human behavior: You replicate what you celebrate. Positive feedback goes a long way in reinforcing the behavior again. Your kids will likely continue to do what you reward them for doing. If I remember correctly, the scientist Ivan Pavlov proved this theory as he trained dogs through positive reinforcement. When we parents celebrate spiritual milestones, we are reinforcing behavior that can be practiced for a lifetime.

Plan your fun

Set aside some time for memory making moments. My mom and dad were big believers in this idea. They made it a point to go on family vacations, and to get out of the routine and make memories. They pointed out that, "Those are the times you will remember. The everyday fun sort of runs together and those memories tend to drift away, but the times you do outside of the routine seem to stick better in our minds." I can attest that looking back on my childhood that they were absolutely right. The out-of-routine memories are the memories that last.

You likely have already discovered ways to play as a family. Each family is unique and you'll find what works for your crew. We discovered that as the kids grew up, their tastes changed and we have had to invent new ways of having fun together.

In Appendix I, we've generated a list of ideas and resources for families that are looking to have some fun and make some memories. Give it a look. Let me challenge you to put your family fun on the calendar. Take a night, a day, or a weekend to laugh, relax and play together.

Fun is foundational

This chapter is buried towards the back of the book (due to the order of the festivals), but it is foundational. If you don't take time to celebrate or if you rarely have fun as a family, it's going to limit how well you lead in all of the other areas. Your kids need to know that they are loved and that you genuinely enjoy their company. Having fun as a family is the love language of every kid. Laughter tears down walls. Being silly makes you safe. Being interested in their interests gives you credibility. And connection needs to be present when there is correction needed. When parents "exasperate" their children (remember Ephesians 6:4?), it is due to a relationship that is all correction and little connection. It just doesn't work. So, don't see this as anything but a big deal. Have fun as a family and watch how God opens doors for you to feel connected and how that strengthens all the other facets of discipling your kids.

How Else Will They Know

Family Discussion:

What is your favorite memory as a family?

What do you dream about doing together in the future?

Kid's Question:

What do you love to do as a family?

Parent Portal:

As you listen to your children answer the above questions, is it possible to see these ideas through?

How might you need to rearrange work or your schedule in order to make this happen?

9 THE DAY OF ATONEMENT

The Lord said to Moses, "The tenth day of this seventh month is the Day of Atonement. Hold a sacred assembly and deny yourselves, and present a food offering to the Lord. Do not do any work on that day, because it is the Day of Atonement, when atonement is made for you before the Lord your God.
Leviticus 23:26–28

The Day of Atonement was a special day with the purpose of reminding each individual person that they had a debt of sin before a holy God that needed to be paid. The purpose of the festival was to atone or cover that sin, so that a right relationship with God could be restored. The ceremony for this day is spelled out in detail in Leviticus 16, and I encourage you to read it. The main ideas of that chapter include the description of several sacrifices:

- The sacrifice of a bull to cover the sins of the High Priest
- The sacrifice of a goat for the sins of the people
- The confession of sin while the High Priest placed his hands on the "scapegoat". The scapegoat was a live goat that was set free, taking the sin of the people away from them into the wilderness.

These sacrifices related to the festival are rich with meaning for us today.

Confession Time

First, let's start with the sacrifice of the bull on behalf of the High Priest. It showed that everyone, including even the High Priest, had a sin debt before God. Being the spiritual leader of your home, or at church, doesn't exempt you from confession of sin to God. In fact, it demands that you do it more. Everyone needs time to evaluate their relationship with God, to admit where they have failed, and confess those sins to God. In your family, confession should start at the top. As the spiritual

How Else Will They Know

leader of your home, you should regularly evaluate how you are doing with the Lord. First lead yourself to regular confession so that you can personally draw near to God.

Let me illustrate this point. If you were making a repair at home and someone offered to take the lead on the project, you would want that person to have experience with that type of repair. If they showed up and told you that they had never done anything like that before, you would quickly find someone else for the repair. So, it is in leading our homes. We have to lead by example. Jesus said it best: The student is not above the teacher, but everyone who is fully trained will be like their teacher. (Luke 6:40) As the "teacher" in your home, set the pace for the rest to follow.

Confession of our sin is directed towards God (1 John 1:9). However, sometimes we also need to confess our sins to others if we have offended them. This includes our family. If our sin was done in front of others, or in public, then we also need to make a public apology in front of these same people. For instance, if you became angry and spoke harshly with someone in front of everyone else, then it is necessary to gather everyone back up and admit that you were out of line to everyone present.

I had an embarrassing example of this a few years back. I had developed a habit of complaining in the car about one person in our family who was usually running behind, while the rest of us waited in the car. It was wrong. I knew it, but knowing it was wrong didn't stop it. Finally, after setting a poor example many times, I realized God was convicting me about this sinful behavior and I repented, confessing my sin to God. Then, the next time this situation came up, it was admittedly a struggle, but I didn't say anything. Then, what I heard from the back seat broke my heart. One of my kids had taken up my complaint where I left off. The very words I had used previously were now being repeated. I knew then that I couldn't only confess this sin to

How Else Will They Know

God, but I had to confess it to my family as well, including the person I had complained about. So, I did. I told them I was wrong for complaining. I told them all that I was sorry that I had given them such a poor example. I asked them to forgive me and to not repeat the same mistake. I can tell you this. There isn't much worse than knowing that you have led your family down the wrong path.

Secondly, the Day of Atonement was an annual reminder of the seriousness of sin. The animals were slaughtered because sin always has a cost. Just like in the animal sacrifices used in festival worship, our sin always has a cost associated with it. It often costs us far more than we realize. God has revealed that "the wages of sin is death" (Romans 6:23) and that "we reap what we sow" (Galatians 6:7). Those passages are warnings to stay away from sin because the cost is great.

Finally, don't miss that this festival reveals the grace of God. God in His goodness chooses to remove the sins from His people by providing a "scapegoat". This is a preview of the coming Savior. God's grace is fully realized in the death and resurrection of Jesus, removing our sins "once for all" (1 Peter 3:18). By removing our sin, God made it possible for us to have an intimate relationship with Him.

In summary, the Day of Atonement is an example of how we are to continue to grow in our relationship with God through avoiding sin, confessing sin, and growing in our appreciation of God's grace. It is a call to intimacy with God and spiritual growth. And the first step of helping your kids grow spiritually is to grow yourself. How are you doing with that? Is spending time with God in worship, confession, prayer, Bible reading and the like a part of your lifestyle? If so, you are setting the right example by leading yourself well and that qualifies you to lead your family. If not, make these things a habit in your life, even as you begin to lead your family in them as well.

How Else Will They Know

I said earlier that there isn't much worse than knowing you have led your family down the wrong road, but the opposite is also true. There isn't anything better than leading them down the right path. The best thing you can do for your family is to fall in love with God, to seek Him, and to help them to do the same. This is spiritual leadership. Since we have this privilege, the remainder of this chapter will look at practical ways in which we can grow, and help our family grow closer to God.

The following list of "spiritual disciplines" are timeless practices that have the purpose of drawing us near to God. None of the following are new practices, but I wanted to make them memorable for kids in the "digital age" so I have given them contemporary titles.

Alerts

I've realized that there are two kinds of people in the world - those who can't stand having unattended alerts at the top of their phone, and those who *always* have unchecked alerts covering the top of their phones. If you haven't guessed by now, I'm one of the former types. Alert icons drive me nuts! I'm hoping to find a support group for this problem. Regardless of how you roll, it's important that we don't miss God's work in our lives by not attending to the disciplines of spiritual growth He has given to us. The following timeless practices we'll call "alerts" are how we grow in our relationship with God. The analogy of phone alerts can be helpful in understanding and practicing the spiritual disciplines that are a means to spiritual growth.

Missed calls

It is so ironic that most people over the age of twelve in our tech-savvy world walk around with a cell phone, but the one thing they do the least on their devices is to actually call someone. A friend called my youngest daughter one time and she answered the phone by asking, "Why are you calling me? You have text!" And as convenient as texting is, when you really need somebody, you call. Calling on God in conversation is

How Else Will They Know

called prayer. Prayer is a beautiful gift God has given us that we can talk to Him in any given moment. The Psalmist said,

> *"I call on you, my God, for you will answer me; turn your ear to me and hear my prayer." Psalm 17:6*

We can and should pray to God all the time, about all kinds of things. Jesus gave us a model prayer:

> *"This, then, is how you should pray:*
>
> *" 'Our Father in heaven,*
>
> *hallowed be your name,*
>
> *your kingdom come,*
>
> *your will be done,*
>
> *on earth as it is in heaven.*
>
> *Give us today our daily bread.*
>
> *And forgive us our debts,*
>
> *as we also have forgiven our debtors.*
>
> *And lead us not into temptation,*
>
> *but deliver us from the evil one.'" Matthew 6:9-13*

According to this model prayer, when we make the call to God, we should include four elements: praise, requests, confession, and yielding to Him. Praise is seen in the phrase, "hallowed be your name". It is giving God the credit He deserves for who He is and for what He has done. We see Jesus' modeling praying for requests when He prays,

How Else Will They Know

"Give us today our daily bread." It is good to ask God for things - for both yourself and for others. We should pray for healing, that God would provide, for strength to face difficulty, and a great number of other things. Jesus also models a prayer of confession by praying, "And forgive us our debts." While Jesus had no debt before a holy God, we certainly will. Confession is admitting that you have missed God's will for you. When we acknowledge where we have been wrong, we tell God we are sorry and ask for His help to not do so again. When we do so, He promises to forgive and restore intimate fellowship with us (see 1 John 1:9) Finally, we yield our lives to God as we pray, "Your will be done." That simple prayer means that God knows best, so we will seek to live by the standards of His Word through the power given to us by His Spirit. You will grow as you make each of these a part of your own personal prayer life. Model them to your family by including them in prayers together. I'm a believer that you don't learn about prayer from Bible study and instruction nearly as much as you do by simply praying. Pray together as a family.

I also believe that God has given us emotions for many reasons, and one of them is to alert us to pray. The alerts of worry, fear, and anger, to name a few, are signals for us to pray. When they go off, pray. Do this with your kids. When they are upset, take time to listen, then pray with them.

There are so many ways in which to grow in prayer that it will be overwhelming to try to tackle that here. But I will suggest one practice. Write down your family prayer requests. Then, when you see God answer them, write that down next to the request. Over the years, you'll be able to see the hand of God at work and it will strengthen everyone's resolve to "pray and not give up" (Luke 18:1). We have included a sample "family prayer journal" in Appendix J.

How Else Will They Know

A few years ago, I started the year by listing seven specific prayer requests in the back of my Bible that I asked God to answer. Those requests ranged from direction for my family, to providing financially, to ministry goals, just to name a few. Over the course of that single year, I saw a specific and clear answer to five of those seven requests. It is such a faith building exercise to see God respond to prayer!

So, what does your prayer life look like? Are you in the habit of talking with God on a daily basis? Do you worship Him in prayer? Do you confess your sins to Him? Do you lay out requests before Him for you and for others? Do you pray for His fame to grow on earth? May each of us grow in prayer. May we be known as people of prayer. Let's be intentional about leading our families to pray - pray together at meals, as situations arise, and in intercession for others.

Unread mail

God has sent you His very words, the scriptures. For some, email may be a bad analogy because you have at least 3,284 unread emails in your inbox. Regardless of how you are doing with your inbox, the truth remains that God is trying to communicate to you daily through His Word. God is sending you mail every day. Don't miss it. Make it your intention and habit to read the Bible every day. Some days, that means you will read it out of duty and habit. That's okay. Don't stop reading it just because it doesn't come easy or without sacrifice. As you do, you'll find that you enter into seasons of life where reading God's Word takes on a new dynamic - it becomes a joy. You get to the place where you can say like the Psalmist:

> I delight in your decrees; I will not neglect your word.
> Psalm 119:16

There are foundational truths about God's Word that help it become a joy. When you believe that the Bible isn't simply a book but God talking directly to you, it becomes a joy. When you see the trouble and pain

How Else Will They Know

that you avoid by obeying it, it becomes a joy. When it lifts your soul when you're down, God's Word becomes a joy! When God's Word helps you like that, then you can't wait to get to your "inbox" and see what God has to say.

As with all the other disciplines, be sure to lead yourself first. Spend time in God's Word. Your time with God is not primarily about learning new things, but to meet in communion with God and to have his Word "renew your mind" (Romans 12:2). Here's how to get the most out of your Bible reading:

- Read the Bible expecting God to communicate with you. When a verse gets your attention by "jumping off the page" that is something you need to stop and pay attention to.
- Pray about what that verse is saying. Ask how God wants you to see that verse applied to your life.
- Look for a truth to believe, a sin to confess, an attitude to change, or an action to take.
- As God leads you to action, put it on your calendar or "to do list". Don't let it fade away with good intentions and not follow through with action.

Recently I saw a great example of this. A woman named Ellen in our church contacted me. She said, "Is there someone who has a financial need in our church?" I asked her why she asked that question and she responded, "Because during my time in God's Word, He impressed on me that my husband and I need to be willing to share some of our resources with someone in need." Talk about finding specific ways to take action! I thank God that He speaks specifically to us and that if we are listening in His Word, we can discern what He wants us to do.

Backlogged texts

Have you ever counted how many texts you get a day? I'm guessing I

How Else Will They Know

just lost some of you because you went to count! If so, welcome back. Texts are now a part of our lives in a significant way. They are so convenient. They are great for in-the-moment communication, quick hitters, and reminders. They provide us with "just in time communication". That's a great way to describe the role of the Holy Spirit in the life of a believer. The Spirit of God lives inside every believer (Ephesians 1:13) and is a constant presence in our lives. As the Psalmist said:

> Where can I go from your Spirit? Where can I flee from your presence? Psalm 139:7

The Spirit is always with us, prompting us, directing and empowering us just when we need Him. He is the voice of God communicating to us and leading us as we go through our days. Our attitude towards God's Spirit is to be like the Psalmist:

> Teach me to do your will, for you are my God; may your good Spirit lead me on level ground. Psalm 143:10

How aware are you of the Holy Spirit's role in your life? Do you respond to his prompting, reminding, convicting, and comfort? Hopefully you have and are experiencing this in your life regularly. It is something we grow in throughout our whole lives. The activity of the Spirit is how we take what we hear in prayer, learn in Bible study, discuss in small groups, are convicted about in preaching and then flesh it out in our daily lives.

Leading your family to be sensitive to the leadership of the Holy Spirit can be tricky. A lot of us are still figuring it out, so it's hard to explain to someone else. But to start, help them recognize the leadership of the Holy Spirit. When they are convicted about something they have done wrong, let them know that that was the Spirit. When they are moved with compassion, help out someone, or otherwise serve God, teach them that the person of the Spirit was responsible for those desires.

97

How Else Will They Know

When they are faced with quick decisions or temptations, teach your kids to shoot a quick "text" to God in prayer and then to listen to the Spirit of God in their hearts and minds. Seek to use real life situations to teach them reliance on and submission to the Spirit of God. And like everything else, modeling is key.

There were times when our children were younger that the demands of raising three small children seemed overwhelming to my wife and I. Maybe you can relate. I should have been relying on the leadership of the Spirit instead of trying to do things myself, but in reality, I wasn't. It was in a moment of frustration I realized I had hit my limit. I sensed God was asking me to rely on Him instead. So, I threw up my hands in a dramatic fashion and prayed out loud (in my best preacher voice), "Lord Jesus give me strength". It was a real prayer, but done in a way that broke the tension in the home and the hardness of my own heart. The old saying goes, "you either laugh or you cry". The Spirit led us to laughter and reliance on Him. In the years that followed, when I sensed my frustration level rising, I would pray that prayer out loud. It did wonders for me. That quick "text" prayer was the difference between being frustrated by my own limitations and letting God lead me with His limitless resources.

Use "just in time communication" between yourself and God. Occasionally pray your "quick hitter" prayers out loud so that your kids can hear what they look like. My kids have heard me pray for patience more than once behind the wheel. It shows I'm broken and in need of the Lord's help. It models what relying on the Spirit really looks like.

Broken streaks

Do you have snapchat? I don't, but I realized that everyone under twenty years old does! The whole concept is really lost on me, but my basic understanding is that if you communicate back and forth with someone every day you keep your streak with them alive. I watch my kids take pictures of the most random things and send it - taillights, trees, anything really. The content apparently isn't that important, but the daily "touch" is. The same is true with growing in relationship with God. God wants to get a "touch" with you every day. The Psalmist declares:

> *"Then I will ever sing in praise of your name and fulfill my vows day after day." Psalm 61:8*

The key to growing in intimacy with God is consistency, seeking Him on a daily basis. Now, I'm not saying that if we miss a day with God, that we are in any way "starting over", but I am suggesting that as we get into a rhythm of a daily quiet time with God, it builds the relationship like nothing else.

Having unlimited access to God is something, quite frankly, that I know I take for granted. But that wasn't always the case. Look at how the Day of Atonement reveals the grace and gift of God being accessible to us.

> *The Lord said to Moses: "Tell your brother Aaron that he is not to come whenever he chooses into the Most Holy Place behind the curtain in front of the atonement cover on the ark, or else he will die. Leviticus 16:2*

Access to God in that day only happened in the Holy of Holies (a small part of the tabernacle and then later the temple), but it was restricted to once a year for one man, the High Priest, on this Day of Atonement. One man, once a year, that's it. That's how it was. Then Jesus died for all the sins of the world. And when He did, the scriptures show a new access to God.

> *And when Jesus had cried out again in a loud voice, he gave up his spirit. At that moment the curtain of the temple was torn in two from top to bottom. The earth shook, the rocks split. Matthew 27:50–51*

How Else Will They Know

The moment that Jesus died, the curtain that shielded people from the presence of God in the Holy of Holies was torn. The perfect man, Jesus, obeyed God by dying in our place. The sin that separated us from God was removed. God ripped the curtain open as an invitation to all as if saying, "Come to me. I'm accessible now. You don't have to go through another man. You aren't restricted to once a year. Now anyone anywhere at any time can come to me through Jesus." God is inviting us all to come near to Him. You and I need God as a vital part of our daily lives. Our families need you to be near Him. You can't lead them down the right path without staying near Him. Let that motivate you. May you enjoy a rich and regular time with your God.

To lead your kids to have a quiet time with God is one of the greatest gifts you can give them. But like most of these leadership responsibilities, it requires leading from the side. I am not a believer in forcing them to spend a quiet time. I do believe we need to equip them to know how to have one, to pray that they will want to know God better (Ephesians 1:17), and to remind them that God wants to spend time with them. To equip them, we need to show them how. We need to teach them some principles about why you have a quiet time, what to do in that time, and of course, to model it for them.

With each of my kids, I dedicated one morning a week before school for a whole school year to invest in each one of them in this way. Sometime during the middle school years works great. I found that buying them a biscuit was all the motivation that they needed! By then they are usually able to read and comprehend what they read in God's Word, process it, and respond back to God. Those mornings invested in my kids are some of my fondest memories. We took time to read the book "Feeding Your Soul" by Jean Fleming, published by NavPress. Then, we would discuss what we read. After that, we would read the same section of scripture separately, working through one of the Gospels. We would have our "quiet times" on the same passage. Then, we would pray about what we read, sometimes journal our thoughts, or

How Else Will They Know

write out a prayer to God, all while sitting across the table from each other, but not interrupting one another. Then, I would read what I wrote to them, and ask them if they wanted to share what they had written. They always did. Honestly, I got emotional listening to their prayers written back to God, realizing they had heard from Him and were seeking to live for Him.

That was my plan. It may not be the best plan or what you decide to do, but I do urge you to have a plan. Be intentional about teaching your kids how to spend time with God. If you give them that one gift, it has the greatest potential for them living for God than any other thing I can think of. In chapter 11, you'll be crafting your own plan for your family and each individual child. I'll encourage you to start praying now for what God wants for your children in this area.

How Else Will They Know

Family Discussion:

How important is it to you to spend time with God? If that is a habit you are having trouble with, what is getting in the way?

Kid's Question:

What do you think about God wanting to spend time with you?

Parent Portal:

Are you growing in your practice of having a quiet time?

What action steps will you take to help your children experience meaningful time with God?

How Else Will They Know

10 THE FESTIVAL OF TABERNACLES

Celebrate the Festival of Tabernacles for seven days after you have gathered the produce of your threshing floor and your winepress. Be joyful at your festival - you, your sons and daughters, your male and female servants, and the Levites, the foreigners, the fatherless and the widows who live in your towns. For seven days celebrate the festival to the Lord your God at the place the Lord will choose. For the Lord your God will bless you in all your harvest and in all the work of your hands, and your joy will be complete. Deuteronomy 16:13–15

At first glance the Festival of Tabernacles is similar to many of the other festivals in the Jewish calendar, in that it consists of eight days of feasts, rejoicing, and burnt offerings. Here, Israel is celebrating the last harvest of the year, the grain harvest. As such, it is the culmination of all the celebrations and perhaps the crescendo of ancient Jewish worship each year. The ancient historian, Josephus claimed that the Feast of Booths (another name for the festival) was the preeminent ancient Israelite celebration.[11] So, while the magnitude of this festival cannot be overstated, it is the subtle differences to the other festivals where we will find some unique lessons to be learned for all of Israel and all of us. Other passages reveal the distinctive teachings found in the Festival of Tabernacles. One passage is found in Leviticus.

On the first day you are to take branches from luxuriant trees— from palms, willows and other leafy trees—and rejoice before the LORD your God for seven days. Celebrate this as a festival to

---

[11] Rooker, M. F. (2000). Leviticus (Vol. 3A, p. 290). Nashville: Broadman & Holman Publishers.

the LORD for seven days each year. This is to be a lasting ordinance for the generations to come; celebrate it in the seventh month. Live in temporary shelters for seven days: All native-born Israelites are to live in such shelters so your descendants will know that I had the Israelites live in temporary shelters when I brought them out of Egypt. I am the LORD your God. Leviticus 23:40–43

In order to remember their journey from Egypt to the Promised Land that they now occupied, God commanded all of Israel to live in temporary shelters for this week, hence the name "tabernacles" or "booths". Talk about an object lesson. Our family can barely stomach a night in the tent in the backyard. Sleeping on the ground isn't all it's cracked up to be! The Jewish people passed down this instruction from God for generations and even reinstated it after the exile into Babylon during the days of Nehemiah.

So the people went out and brought back branches and built themselves temporary shelters on their own roofs, in their courtyards, in the courts of the house of God and in the square by the Water Gate and the one by the Gate of Ephraim. The whole company that had returned from exile built temporary shelters and lived in them. Nehemiah 8:16–17

It was also during the Festival of Tabernacles that Solomon dedicated the temple to the Lord, moved the ark of the covenant into the Most Holy Place, and assembled Israel to worship God. The account of this event can be found in 1 Kings chapter 8.

Gratitude (Yes, again)

What exactly was God communicating to His people during this week of "slumming it"? Gratitude. He wanted people who were not entitled or forgetful, but for them to always remember how far God had brought them now that they possessed the land and were living off its abundance. One commentator remarked: "The festival is somewhat comparable to the American celebration of Thanksgiving."[12] That assessment is fitting considering that the festival incorporates:

- Remembering the faithfulness of God in delivering them from bondage
- Their journey to freedom
- God's provision along the way
- The establishing of the people of Israel as a nation
- God's faithfulness to bless them in agricultural abundance.

That sounds a lot like the Pilgrims who came to the Americas. They celebrated the first Thanksgiving as a people who were grateful for a journey across the vast ocean, who endured a bitter winter, who gained an alliance with the natives, and who were grateful for the crops that produced an abundance.

A Bigger Story

In chapter 6, the Festival of Firstfruits, we covered how to lead from the side to help cultivate gratitude in our children. So, let's look at this from a different angle. For the children experiencing the Festival of Tabernacles and the children who understand the significance of Thanksgiving, both of them are being connected through those experiences to the bigger story of God. The Jewish girl would know that the God she prays to is the same God who preserved the lives of her ancestors in a desert for decades, who parted the sea, and who delivered His people. The boy who celebrates the bounty of Thanksgiving in its original context knows that God had provided, worked miracles, and established His people of faith on a new

---

[12] Rooker, M. F. (2000). Leviticus (Vol. 3A, p. 291). Nashville: Broadman & Holman Publishers.

How Else Will They Know

continent. Both will ultimately see the bigger picture that

their lives are not a single strand, but that the thread of their lives is being woven into a larger tapestry in the story of God.

I can imagine individual families passing along their own unique "tabernacle stories" down from one generation to the next, recounting the specific ways God had been faithful to them. It might sound like this in a Hebrew household:

"Great grandfather Eli had a pair of sandals that he walked out of Egypt in and they lasted him the rest of his life"

"And your great Aunt Sarah wore the same dress the entire time they lived in that desert and it never had to be mended"

"God provided meat and a delicious flaky bread to eat for all of us. Your mother makes the best quail pie!"

"Isn't God great that He would care for His people, our people, *your* people like that?"

Now the little girl hearing these stories is connected to the grand story of God. The God of her ancestors is her God too. That's part of what is being conveyed as God describes himself as "The God of Abraham, Isaac, and Jacob" (See Exodus 6:2-3). That connects all of Israel to the patriarchs, to the God of miracles, and the God who shaped history.

And that is what we should intend to do for our children as well - connect them to the eternal story of God. As their parents we have our own "God stories" to tell. Take time to write down the account of the times when God "came through" for you. This should be a living document that you keep adding to as God proves His faithfulness to you time and again. We can also connect them to other heroes - stories of faith of their ancestors, major figures in the history of Christianity, and Christians around the world. We want them to sense a connection to

How Else Will They Know

the story of God, the history of the church, and a bond with the universal church spread across the globe. To be honest, I have only recently discovered the power of connecting my kids to the bigger story of God. This is one I am playing serious catch-up on. Yet, I want them to know that God's plan has been unfolding since the foundation of the world and will continue long after we are gone (assuming Christ delays His return). I believe this will stir in them a sense of belonging, knowing they are part of something vast and important. I believe it will tie them to the faith when other outside factors will challenge what they believe, particularly when they move out on their own one day. I believe they will see their lives as a link in a long chain of faith, as they realize their own role in passing on the faith to their generation and the next generation. There are likely other benefits beyond this, but like I said, I'm new to this one. Let's just say that connecting kids to the bigger story of God looks to be a big win.

Here are some practical ideas on how to connect them to the bigger story of God.

- Listen to famous messages of past generations.
- Read biographies of prominent believers.
- Familiarize them with key figures from Christian history.
- Look up the story behind powerful hymns and theologically rich songs of today.
- Get connected with mission organizations so you can learn stories of missionaries around the world.
- Discuss what it would be like to be a believer during the early church, during medieval times, in the midst of the protestant reformation or being first-hand during one of the Great Awakenings.

Our family is very musical. All three of our children excelled in the school band program. Two of them were in marching band in high school. My wife and daughters sing beautifully, using the gifts God has given them in the school chorus and our church worship band. It is a rare moment when someone in this house isn't singing. Guess who the odd guy out is? This guy! Anyway, since there is such a love for worshipping God through song in our family, we shared the story of the classic hymn "Amazing Grace" with our kids. You may know it already, but it is worth repeating. So here goes.

One Example

In 1745, John Newton was enlisted in the slave trade, running captured slaves from Africa to Charleston, S.C. His profession made him wealthy through the selling of people he viewed as property and he seemingly had little regard for as human beings. Then in 1748, he found himself in a violent storm at sea where he was certain he would lose his life. It was in this moment of crisis that he found his faith.[13]

That day in the storm, March 21, 1748, was a day Newton remembered ever after, for "On that day the Lord sent from on high and delivered me out of deep waters." Many years later, as an old man, Newton wrote in his diary of March 21, 1805: "Not well able to write; but I endeavor to observe the return of this day with humiliation, prayer, and praise." Only God's amazing grace could and would take a rude, profane, slave-trading sailor and transform him into a child of God. Newton never ceased to stand in awe of God's work in his life.[14]

It was this profound work of God's grace that transformed John Newton into a child of God. It was that grace that inspired him to write, "Amazing Grace". It was that grace that transformed a willing participant in slave trade to become an advocate for the abolishment of

---

[13] Time.com, "The Incredible True story behind 'Amazing Grace'", June 28th, 2015.

[14] Christianity Today.com, "John Newton Discovered Amazing Grace", April 28th, 2010.

slavery. The words of that hymn become even more powerful and inspiring when we know that the author had experienced this grace in such a profound way.

The story of John Newton is just one example. Appendix K has a list of Christian heroes and corresponding resources so that you can discover their story together as a family. So, take one at a time. Don't feel like you have to do them all. Don't race through the list. It is better to let a few impactful stories sink in than to brush past them all. And at the same time, don't let that list restrain you from discovering so much more in our rich heritage of faith. If your family takes to this part of the discipleship plan, then the sky's the limit. Regardless, endeavor to pass on, "the faith that was once for all entrusted to God's holy people" (Jude 3). The more we do so, the more likely the next generation will be to see following Jesus as something that transcends culture, language, circumstances, and race and the less likely they will see their faith as something that is pigeon-holed into a particular mold formed by their own context.

People of the Word

Another distinct element of the Festival of Tabernacles is the mandatory reading of the Law every seven years to the congregation, young and old alike.

> *Then Moses commanded them: "At the end of every seven years, in the year for canceling debts, during the Festival of Tabernacles, when all Israel comes to appear before the LORD your God at the place he will choose, you shall read this law*

How Else Will They Know

before them in their hearing. Assemble the people—men, women and children, and the foreigners residing in your towns—so they can listen and learn to fear the LORD your God and follow carefully all the words of this law. Their children, who do not know this law, must hear it and learn to fear the LORD your God as long as you live in the land you are crossing the Jordan to possess." Deuteronomy 31:10–13

Can you imagine standing the entire time while someone reads the law of God - like the entire book of Leviticus - out loud? My back starts to grumble after standing for four songs at a worship gathering. Most of us have trouble reading through the Old Testament law on our own while sitting comfortably. Yet, here are the Hebrew people, young and old, healthy and weak, standing at attention for hours. Wow! What a commitment to the Word of God! Knowing they didn't have access to the scriptures individually (and this has been the case for much of history) makes you realize just how blessed we are to have access to it in the Western world today. I wonder if the familiarity and ease of access has spoiled us to not appreciate it as we should.

Reading of God's Word is prominent and necessary for all of us to grow personally, and it is equally crucial to pass on the faith to the next generation. As the spiritual leader in the home, we have the great privilege to get into the scriptures with our families. This will certainly mean reading God's Word together. It will include studying topics and books of the Bible together. It could mean memorizing scripture together. In short, it will require you to develop a habit of having what we call a "family devo" (devotional).

The Devo

First of all, let me calm some fears about leading your family in the scriptures. You don't have to have a Bible degree or seminary training. You don't need to have all the answers. It is perfectly fine to admit that there are things that you yourself don't understand and that frankly,

How Else Will They Know

you are having trouble obeying. What you do need to have is intentionality. The pace of the modern family is astounding. With so many choices in entertainment, recreation, and social opportunities, the one thing the spiritual leader must do is create a time for the family to gather around the Bible and meet with God together. As our kids have gotten older, this has become a bigger and bigger challenge. When they were younger, we would often do this weekly. Now, we do it less frequently, but still with intentionality. A couple times a month, we have our "devo" together.

Once your family is gathered, have a plan for your reading. You can read through a book of the Bible together. You can study a Biblical figure. You can study a topic that they are interested in. You can read a devotional together. Resources abound for just such a gathering. The YouVersion Bible app has a ton of resources included in it. Whatever you choose, make sure that the scriptures have a prominent role. Don't read a short snippet of God's Word and a ton of commentary. What you and your family need is to hear the Word of God, just like the Israelites standing at attention.

As you engage with God's truth, discuss what you have read. Ask the family what they thought of the passage. Ask them what stood out to them. Ask them what they didn't understand. Ask them one thing they want to do in response to what they have read. Share with them your answers as well. Just don't dominate the conversation. Don't allow someone else to dominate the conversation either. This needs to be a good "give and take" situation. Use this time to help them think Biblically about God, themselves, the people around them, and the world they live in. A healthy discussion will give you plenty of teachable moments, unearth some uncomfortable (but transformative) issues, and help all of you to grow. Admittedly, this takes some practice to refine, but don't let a lack of experience keep you from getting started. I have found that my family (and likely yours too) will be gracious about any lack of preparation, stumbling through the passage, or poorly worded questions. They may not say it, but they do appreciate you caring enough to lead them in their spiritual growth. Trust me on this. I have been thanked very little over the years, but if we go too long in having a "family devo" inevitably someone will ask me when we are going to have another.

Try it. Don't try to make it last too long. In fact, the younger your kids are, the shorter the devotional time needs to be. I recommend no longer than 5 minutes for preschoolers, 15 minutes for grade schoolers, 30 minutes for middle schoolers, and 45 minutes for high schoolers. Don't worry about covering a lot of territory, instead focus on creating the habit. In addition to reading the scripture and discussing it, it is a good practice to ask how they are doing and how you can be praying for each other. It is powerful when your spouse or kids open up about something on their heart and ask for prayer from the family. Being vulnerable yourself goes a long way in giving permission for the rest of the crew to be transparent themselves. Once you've talked over these concerns, pray. Pray about what you read. Pray for each other. It may be only you praying at first, but encourage others to join you in praying over the months and years. Creating a safe place to pray out loud at home gives your kids boldness to be able to pray in public with others. It makes it a very normal thing to do. The earlier you start this practice, the easier it seems to be to pray out loud in front of other people. Starting young helps your children realize that prayer isn't about "sounding good" but simply being real with God. There is little that makes you smile more than when you hear your child praying to God sincerely. Any effort it takes to work towards this end seems like a small sacrifice when you hear them praying to their Savior!

Getting Started

If your kids are young enough, you can just jump right in. Sit them down and have the first family devotional together. It won't be perfect, but it is a beginning. Just have a plan for what you will read before you begin.

How Else Will They Know

If your kids are older, or if you think you'll get resistance from someone in the family, then I suggest that you first have a quick "family meeting" explaining what you would like to do. Most people don't like having things dropped on them at the last minute. Giving a heads up goes a long way to share your excitement and expectations as you prepare them for what is coming. Tell them what you intend to do, ask for feedback, and then set up your first "family devo" as people check their schedules.

In Appendix L, we have created a list of resources you can use for your family devotional time. It is a good place to start. I highly encourage starting with one of these if this is new to you. Eventually, you will want to set the agenda according to what your family needs. Ultimately, you want to see your family so invested in this practice, that they are shaping the direction for what you read and how you care for each other. Now that is what God had in mind for the family to be a catalyst for spiritual growth!

What are you waiting for? Start that family devo! How else will they know?

How Else Will They Know

Family Discussion:

- What questions do you have about God or the Bible?
- Are you interested in a Bible character or book of the Bible?
- What issues are you facing that you want to have God's perspective on?

Kid's Question:

How do you like to learn - stories? Reading? Visuals? Videos? Something else?

Parent Portal:

What steps do you need to take to get your family in the scriptures together? How will you prepare to lead in this way? When will you start?

How Else Will They Know

11 CRAFTING YOUR PLAN

In this final chapter, you can put together all that we have discovered into a practical, doable plan for you and your family. Just think, you can have a game plan for discipling your children. It won't be fool-proof. It won't be perfect. It may even seem a bit overwhelming, but you'll have a place to start and an end in mind.

If I could do it all over again, I would include my whole family in the planning process. I would introduce an idea presented in one of these chapters (let's say family devo) and ask them what they wanted to learn or study. When they are little, you might be steering the discussion significantly, but at least they would have input and buy-in into the plan as well. As you construct your plan, there are several factors to keep in mind.

Age graded

An obvious factor to your approach is the age of your children. We think the following age categories are helpful in planning: preschool (ages 0-5), elementary (ages 6-10), middle school (ages 11-14), and high school (ages 15-18). Following the lead of our education system, these categories take advantage of how children learn, read, and process information. The plan must be adapted according to the development of your children.

The age of your children will determine the depth of Bible study you can do. It will influence how intense and long a ministry opportunity should be. It impacts how penetrating a question you can ask them about their own personal holiness or practice of a quiet time. It is your job to determine how much is just right to push them but not discourage them. Remember Ephesians 6:4:

> *Fathers, do not exasperate your children; instead, bring them up in the training and instruction of the Lord.*

We want to see them grow and learn, but not at the expense of damaging their soul. May we all seek God's leadership in the delicate balance between developing but not discouraging.

It is essential that a child's stage of development play into the plan. Let's test this out on something simple like reading scripture together. In the preschool category, clearly the parent is doing the reading. At the elementary age, again the parent is likely to read, but the children can help out and read some simple sections or some key words. I recommend using a "children's Bible" up through the grade school ages since they are easier to understand. By middle school, the average student is able to read a significant amount of the scriptural vocabulary (depending on the translation), with some help given by the adult. It is during this stage of development that you can transition to a modern Bible translation like the New International Version (NIV). Finally, by high school, your child will most likely be able to read scripture unencumbered by reading limitations. If you have children in different stages of development, you will have to manage that in a couple of ways - either alternating between the two types of reading materials, or trying to compromise in the middle. Experiment and settle on what works for your family.

The progression of involving your children more over time is modeled by Jesus in how He trained his disciples. It has been codified as the "Leadership Square".

How Else Will They Know

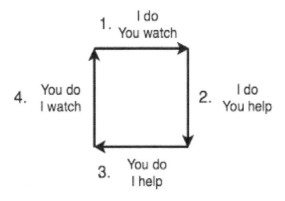

The first step is "I do, you watch" (preschool age).

The second step is "I do, you help" (elementary age).

The third step is "You do, I help" (middle school age).

The final step is "You do, I watch" (high school age).

Engage the whole person

As stated before, discipleship is a "whole person" process. Traditional discipleship methods have targeted the development of people through increased knowledge. And while this is a viable part of maturing in Christ, it falls woefully short on its own. Authentic disciple-making must engage people on multiple levels. Jesus made this clear in his famous statement found in Matthew 22:37.

> *"Love the Lord your God with all your heart and with all your soul and with all your mind."*

According to Jesus, discipleship includes teaching our children to love God with their minds by exposing them to the truths of God and helping them to think critically about how it relates to their lives. It also includes engaging them in the affections of their heart, resulting in convictions about what they believe. And finally, it must impact their soul, which is the place of their will, and results in decisions that shape how they talk, what they do, and what they won't do. All three of these elements combined together comprise loving God as God intended. Later in this chapter we will flesh out this concept through the family discipleship plan template included.

The PLACE factor

One of the tools that our church (and therefore our family) uses to understand how God has wired us is PLACE Ministries' PLACE Assessment.[15] This assessment and the ensuing process of unpacking the results is a powerful tool to know your personality, spiritual gifts, passions, abilities and how you were shaped by life experiences. This small investment helps in a variety of ways. When our kids were in middle school, we had our kids complete the assessment. It helped us to see our kids more clearly and confirmed many things we intuitively knew about them. Secondly, it has helped us have conversations with them about topics like career choices, college, and relationships. Third, it has helped us find a fit in ministry for them in our church and youth group. We discussed this benefit previously in chapter 7. You can purchase a hard copy or online version of the Student PLACE assessment on the PLACE website. See Appendix H for the free app to get started.

Another advantage of using a tool like PLACE is the ability it gives you to tailor the family discipleship plan specifically for each child. I'm sure your house is like mine. No two kids are the same. In fact, they can be so different you wonder how two people can produce two totally different kids! Because your kids are fundamentally different in many ways, you should adjust your plans for discipling them accordingly.

---

[15] Learn more about PLACE at www.placeministries.org/

How Else Will They Know

Where one of our children is highly verbal in their gifts, the other two are more behind the scene servants. Leading them with wisdom makes concessions for such differences and intentionally plays to the strengths each one possesses.

Disabilities

Another factor to consider is when a child has a disability. Consider how you can adjust an activity or creatively go about something for a child who has physical or mental limitations. Let me be clear, those with disabilities are called and capable of being disciples of Jesus as surely as any of us can be with God's help. However, the path they take to get there may need to be catered to them.

So, if you have a child with special needs, adjust the plan accordingly. If your child has ADD or ADHD and has trouble sitting still, don't make sitting still for extended periods of time a hill you choose to die on. Adjust your family devotional to a shorter length. Make the learning more hands-on. For example, while teaching the parable of the sower found in Matthew 13, you could greatly enhance learning and engagement for everyone by getting their fingers dirty as you each touch the type of soils and plants described in that passage. With a little extra planning, preparing for special needs in the family can cause greater creativity and better learning environments for everyone.

If the disability is severe, please afford yourself and your child a lot of grace. You may find yourself in an instance where you simply don't know if your child is getting the message. Continue to persevere. Keep sowing into your child's life. Adjust expectations as needed. Continue to thank God for the gift of a special child. Network with parents of children with a similar condition. Most of all, may you find strength and peace that flows from time spent with the Father.

For further help in this area, I recommend the following resource: How-To Homeschool Your Learning Abled Kid: 75 Questions Answered:

How Else Will They Know

For Parents of Children with Learning Disabilities or Twice Exceptional Abilities, by Sandra K. Cook. Available on Amazon.com.

Time restraints

If you are facing an uphill battle discipling your children because they no longer live with you or you have shared custody, you will need to factor in that challenge also. Again, the goal remains the same - to help our children develop as passionate followers of Jesus - yet the path to get there will need to be altered. You will likely find yourself in one of two scenarios.

The first scenario involves the other parent/guardian being cordial and supportive of developing your children spiritually. If that is the case, give God thanks! I recommend working together in discipling your kids. That means you won't teach all the lessons. It means you'll have to communicate well. It could add some tension (but hopefully not competition) as you both need to do your part. If you can get the other parent to cooperate in this, that is for the best, even if it causes a layer of complication for you. After all, this is about the children's spiritual development. So, pitch the idea and be flexible. The other parent will not do things exactly like you would. That's okay, provided that the instruction is Biblically-based and done in love. You may need to buy two sets of whatever book you are reading together. Whatever practical steps you can take to not put undue pressure on the kids is best.

The second scenario involves the other parent/guardian not being on board with this agenda. That's unfortunate, but should not deter you from following through. You will just have to adjust the pace and your expectations. Doing this without the support of your spouse can make you feel alone. Remember that you are not. Remind yourself of the promise God makes over and over again to those who have faith in

How Else Will They Know

Christ, "I am with you." Find support from your church family, small group members or other people who will be excited that you are passing on your faith to your children.

Don't feel like you have to cram in a whole week's worth of family time into a weekend. Your kids will likely say at some point, "but we don't have to do this when we are at so-and-so's house". Don't let that get you down. While your children will genuinely not want to participate at times (Hey, I'm a pastor and I feel that way once in a while), I believe that overall, children recognize that you are putting in this effort because you care about them and you want the best for them.

I know several divorced families who have to "reprogram" their kids after a week or weekend with the other parent or guardian. Make investing in your children spiritually just another part of the culture that you are creating in your home. My guess is that if you do it in love, it will be something that they embrace over the long-haul.

Putting it All Together

As the cliche states, "Seeing is believing". We have been in the world of ideas for 10 and a half chapters and it is now time to put our plan on paper so we can see what a workable plan will look like. As an example, I have recorded the highlights of our family discipleship plan over the years. It is important to note that what is listed below heavily focuses on the content from chapters 6, 7, 9, and 10. The other chapters are equally important, but either a less structured exercise (like encouraging and challenging in holiness) or a habit that is already built into our family (observing the Sabbath as a day of rest and worship). For each age group, we had an overarching goal - understanding Jesus, embracing Jesus, growing with Jesus, and living like Jesus. These were helpful to know what we were working towards as well as how to be praying for our kids.

How Else Will They Know

Your plan will look different. You will emphasize different things, perhaps. You may choose different resources to use. You may feel convicted to only use the Bible and not Bible study resources. That's fine. Make your plan just that - *your* plan. This just gives you a place to begin.

How Else Will They Know

Age	Know? Believe?	Tools	Do?	How? (model)
0-5	**Understand Jesus**			
Preschool	Talk to Jesus	N/A	Develop habit of Prayer	Pray Together
	Biblical Foundations	The church Children's Curriculum / Children's Bible	Understand God's Word	Family Devotionals
6-10	**Embrace Jesus**			
Elementary school	Give their life to Jesus	Steps to Peace with God	Respond to Jesus	Share the Gospel with them
	Character Development	The Church Children's Curriculum / Family Devotional	Use God's Word	Scripture Memory
11-14	**Grow with Jesus**			
Middle school	Identity in Christ	The Search for Significance	Be satisfied in God alone	Read Together
	Develop Personal Quiet Time	Feeding Your Soul	Develop habit of Quiet Time	Quiet Time Together
	Serve Christ	PLACE Assessment	Serve at church	Serve Together
15-18	**Live like Jesus**			
High school	Cultivate Growth	The Purpose Driven Life	Grow as a Disciple	Read as a family
	Share the Gospel	Evangelism Training	Write Testimony & Learn a Tool	Do as a family
	Heart for Multiplication	The Master Plan of Evangelism	Mission Trip	Go with family

How Else Will They Know

Most of what is listed above was described at some point in this book. Take note that this is an age-graded, holistic approach to discipleship that engages heart, mind, and will. We've used this basic plan with all three of our children - two girls and a boy. What isn't included are the one-on-one talks, Bible studies and teachable moments that are specific to each child. You may find it helpful to develop a specific plan for each child, utilizing some common elements as well as some specific to the kid's interests, gifts, and bent. Honestly, I wish I had thought of that before all three of our kids were in this last phase. We could have been more intentional about catering to their growth. Yet, if that seems overwhelming, don't feel pressure to have a unique plan per child. The most important components of developing a plan are God's Word and prayer. Our intent is not to give you a formula, but a guide. Above all, let the Spirit of God guide you on this path. Part of your growth is to seek God in this. Ask, "Lord, how do you want me to disciple my children?" Then listen. Wait. Write down ideas. Talk about it with your family (as appropriate). Hopefully you've been doing some of that as you read this book. Look back at what you underlined, dog-eared, and highlighted in this book. Take insight from notes you placed in the margin. Lean on the Spirit of God to not only craft your plan, but also to give you the flexibility and discipline it takes to spend time on this important role as spiritual leader in the home.

How Else Will They Know

Below is a blank version of the same chart our family used. You may use this as a template for your family.

Family Discipleship Plan Template

Age	Know? Believe?	Tools	Do?	How? (model)
0-5 Preschool				
6-10 Elementary school				
11-14 Middle school				
15-18 High school				

How Else Will They Know

Since we are throwing charts at you, we might as well do another.
Below is a summary of the festivals and sabbath that this book explored
and their relevant applications to leading your family.

Topic/Title	Principles	Action Step
Sabbath	God as priority	Observe a day of worship & rest
Passover	God is holy, rescues	Participate in Communion & share your Testimony
Unleavened Bread	Pursue holiness	Develop character by encouragement & correction
First Fruits	Gratitude & Generosity	Sponsor the needy, Go on a mission trip
Pentecost/Weeks	Serve poor, use gifts	Serve the poor, find your PLACE in ministry
Trumpets	Celebrate and have fun	Make time for fun
Day of Atonement	Personal Growth	Develop a quiet time
Tabernacles	The Word of God	Have a family devotional

This should be a helpful reference to you as you develop your plan.

How Else Will They Know

The Payoff

Let me close with a verse. It is found in 3 John 1:4:

> *"I have no greater joy than to hear that my children are walking in the truth."*

John the apostle wrote this letter to believers whom he had invested in spiritually. The report he got back encouraged him when he heard that they continued in their faith in Jesus after his time with them had ended. And that's the opportunity we each have as a parent, grandparent or guardian. We have a window of opportunity to invest in our children (biological, adopted, or in the faith) and to help them fall in love with Jesus. Can you imagine the joy of seeing your children continue to walk with God long after the years of your greatest influence with them are over? I can't imagine a greater joy. Our hearts will warm with gratitude and joy as our faith gets passed on to the next generation. May God use you to start a chain reaction with your life that creates disciples who in turn make other disciples. Intentionally living your life in such a way will surely receive these words from your Heavenly Father one day, "Well done my good and faithful servant!" (Matthew 25:21)

How Else Will They Know

Let me leave you with a passage that I hope you find as inspiring as I do in investing spiritually in our children:

We will not hide them from their descendants;

we will tell the next generation

the praiseworthy deeds of the LORD,

his power, and the wonders he has done.

He decreed statutes for Jacob

and established the law in Israel,

which he commanded our ancestors

to teach their children,

so the next generation would know them,

even the children yet to be born,

and they in turn would tell their children.

Then they would put their trust in God

and would not forget his deeds

but would keep his commands.   Psalm 78:4–7

How Else Will They Know

Family Discussion:

What ideas do you have for our family plan? When in our schedule can we make time to meet together as a family?

Kid's Question:

Are you ready to follow the lead of the person leading you to grow closer to God?

Parent Portal:

You are on the verge of seeing God change you, your family, and generations to come. Stop and pray now that God will help you put a plan in place, and to help you lead well and make disciples in your home.

EPILOGUE

Your kids are grown. Maybe they have moved out of your house. Now what? Does that mean we can't have a major impact in their lives? Absolutely not! Several of my friends are in the "empty nest" stage of their lives and they are still making a spiritual investment in their adult kids.

One friend of mine makes time to write an email about once per week that he sends to all three of his children. That email is filled with God's Word, encouragement, and words from his heart. He doesn't know if they always read them, but he is being faithful to keep leading well with his family. Another friend sends a short devotional to his wife and daughters from what he is studying personally in God's Word. It's a commitment, but one he gladly keeps, knowing he still has influence for Christ in his family.

Those two examples give me hope that the day my kids move out on their own isn't the end of my influence. May you and I lay the foundation in our children's lives that goes far beyond eighteen years to a lifetime of pointing them to the great and faithful God.

We also may be faced with the reality that our children do not pursue God as we hoped they would. After all, our role is to raise them as best we know how, pray for them, and entrust them to God who loves them far more than we do. If your kids are currently in a season of life where God is not a priority, don't lose heart. You likely had a phase like that too. Don't pressure them. Love and encourage them. Don't beat yourself up either. You and I made mistakes along the way. We have regrets. We likely wish we had been more intentional about leading our families spiritually. Who doesn't?

Let me leave you with the words a friend of mine heard from a licensed Christian counselor. He challenged my friend to "marinade in the 'good

How Else Will They Know

enough' of God's grace". Those are beautiful words because grace is beautiful. Grace is God making up for the gaps in our own lives with His goodness. It is by grace that God saves you from sin. It is by grace that God loves you and accepts you in the midst of your imperfections. And it is by His grace that your children will love God, know Him personally, and live for Him. You and I can trust God to keep pursuing our kids, calling them to Himself. How great is our God!

How Else Will They Know

Appendix A

The Good News

The good news is that there is a Rescuing God who wants to rescue you!

God wants to rescue you for one simple reason - because He loves you. The motivation behind the rescue mission for you is a deep and personal love that God has for you specifically. That motivation is made clear over and over again in God's written communication to us.

> For God so loved the world that he gave his one and only Son, that whoever believes in him shall not perish but have eternal life. John 3:16

> But God demonstrates his own love for us in this: While we were still sinners, Christ died for us. Romans 5:8

The reason for God's rescue is clear - it is motivated by love.

But why do we need rescue? And what is God rescuing us from?

The answers to those questions are sobering. The reality is that we are all selfish and self-serving. We tend to do what we want, what is best for us, and to think of ourselves first. Don't believe me? Here's a simple test. When you look at a group picture, who is the first person you look for? It's yourself! That's in our nature, to be about ourselves. And, if we look good in the picture, it's a good picture. If we look bad in it, then it gets deleted.

While that example seems harmless, the same selfishness in us causes damage in all areas of our lives. Our selfishness leaves us unsatisfied with what we have, it causes conflicts with others, even with people who are closest to us. The bent in us that is all about us is what God calls sin. Here is what God says:

How Else Will They Know

for all have sinned and fall short of the glory of God...
Romans 3:23

But your iniquities have separated you from your God; your sins have hidden his face from you, so that he will not hear.
Isaiah 59:2

The verdict is in. We are all guilty of sin. This isn't a good person or bad person issue. If we compare ourselves to each other, we can conclude that some of us are better than others. But in comparison to God, none of us are good. We all fall short. Is that something you can admit to yourself and to God? You and I fall short of the holy standards of God. And what's worse is that there are consequences for our sin, in this life and for eternity.

For the wages of sin is death...Romans 6:23

What sin results in is death. Death to fulfillment, to relational harmony, to contentment, and so much more. We don't have to look far in our own lives when people have hurt us or we have hurt others because of selfishness. Sin wrecks so many beautiful things. It also results in damage to our relationship with God. The death God describes in this verse ultimately results in an eternal separation from the God who made us and who loves us. That's not what God wants. That's why God did something about it and went on a rescue mission.

The rescue from our sins is possible because of the actions of Jesus. Jesus was God in the flesh. He came to earth, taking the form of a person to deal with our sins. Jesus is unique in that He is the only human that had no sin. Since Jesus had no sin Himself, He could offer Himself as the sacrifice to pay for our sin.

For Christ also suffered once for sins, the righteous for the unrighteous, to bring you to God. 1 Peter 3:18

133

How Else Will They Know

The righteous One, Jesus, paid the death penalty for all sin, including yours. He did it because you could not pay for them yourself on this side of hell. He did it because you and I cannot do enough good to counterbalance our sin. There is simply no way we can work our way into a relationship with God.

> *For it is by grace you have been saved, through faith—and this is not from yourselves, it is the gift of God— not by works, so that no one can boast. Ephesians 2:8–9*

God is shooting straight with us here. We just can't erase the sin problem by trying to do good. None of us can make up for the sin in our own lives. While that news may be offensive, this teaching is also full of hope. Instead of relying on our "goodness" we can look to two other factors - grace and faith.

Grace is God treating us better than we deserve. God could have left us to fend with our own problems and our tragic destiny, but He didn't. God intervened. He sent Jesus to rescue you when He didn't have to. That's grace! It is God doing for us what we cannot do for ourselves.

So how do we access this grace that brings forgiveness and acceptance from God? The answer is faith. Faith means where we put our hope. So rescuing faith is someone that puts their hope in Jesus to rescue them from sin and to bring them into relationship with God, the Heavenly Father. That kind of faith believes Jesus was the Son of God who died for them. That faith believes Jesus rose from the dead, proving He was God and pronouncing the defeat of sin.

That's the good news. Jesus came to rescue you. The question is - what will you do with that news? It isn't enough simply to agree with these facts. The rescue is complete when you act on what God has done for you.

How Else Will They Know

Yet to all who did receive him, to those who believed in his name, he gave the right to become children of God
John 1:12

God is inviting you to respond to the good news. You respond by believing and receiving. Respond by believing that Jesus is who He said He was and what His resurrection proves He is - God in the flesh. Believe that you are in need of rescue and recognize that Jesus died for your sin. Receive Jesus as your one hope. Receive Jesus so you may experience God's forgiveness, and acceptance. Receive Jesus as the leader of your life, seeking to no longer live for your selfish interests, but for what God wants out of gratitude to Him.

To act in faith, you tell God you are ready to make this decision. Feel free to tell God in your own words you are ready for Him to rescue you. If you want some guidance, here is a sample prayer of what you could say. The words are not magical. It is the sincerity of your heart that matters.

> God, I recognize that because of my sin I am in need of rescue. I acknowledge that I can't do anything to fix it. I need Jesus. So, I am placing my faith in Jesus - as the One who paid for my sin. I receive Jesus as the leader of my life, turning from my life of sin and desiring to please God and to obey Him. Thank you, God, for what you have done for me. I love you. Thank you for loving me first. Amen.

Congratulations! You made the best decision you could ever make! God is pleased with your faith in Him. You now have a relationship with God. He is your Heavenly Father and you are His child. There are many promises God has given about this new relationship, but I'll share one of my favorites:

How Else Will They Know

I give them eternal life, and they shall never perish; no one will snatch them out of my hand. John 10:28

God promises that you now possess eternal life. He gave it as a gift to you when you received Jesus by faith. God also says that the gift can never be taken away from you. Notice that it is not your "grip" on God that guarantees eternal life, but God's "grip" on you. He has you in His hands now, and NOTHING can pull you from His grasp.

How Else Will They Know

Appendix B

Impact Ministries

The *"Essentials Series"* is an excellent resource for those who are new in their relationship with God or those who have been a believer for some time. Here is a brief description of each of the books in the series:

Faith Essentials
(7 weeks)

What we believe about...
Bible; God; Jesus; The Holy Spirit; Man; Salvation; Eternity

Spiritual Growth Essentials
(6 weeks)

Spiritual Disciplines

Assurance; Baptism; Quiet Time; Prayer; Studying God's Word; Spirit-controlled living

Bible Essentials
(8 weeks)

A Survey of the Bible
The Law; History books; Wisdom books; The prophets; The gospels and Acts; The Epistles; Revelation

Church Essentials
(6 weeks)

Understanding God's Church
Its purpose; Its functions; Its strategy; Its structure; Its location

Life Essentials
(7 weeks)

Understanding Your Life Mission
Being a disciple rightly related to God, self, and others; Building disciples by going, baptizing and teaching

Discipleship Essentials
(8 weeks)

Living by the Conduct of Christ

An M-7 Disciple: Member, Magnifier, Minister, Manager, Maturing, Messenger and Multiplier

Ministry Essentials
(5 weeks)

Following the Model of Jesus in Ministry
Be equipped to Reach out, Plug in, Build up, and Send out

How Else Will They Know

Purchase these at: https://impactdisciples.com/product-category/disciple-making-essentials-series/

The **"Impact Series"** is an advanced curriculum designed to help you live by the character and conduct of Jesus and to prepare you to lead like Jesus did. Here is the description of each of the books in the series:

Impact One	Essentials Books
	Spiritual Growth; Faith; Bible; and Life
(28 weeks)	*Essentials*
Impact Two	The Character of Christ
(11 weeks)	*Developing the Fruit of the Spirit in your life*
Impact Three	The Conduct of Christ
(26 weeks)	*Being an M-7 Disciple*
Impact Four	315 Leadership Training
(9 weeks)	*Being a leader after God's Heart*

Purchase these at: https://impactdisciples.com/product-category/impact-series/

How Else Will They Know

Taking Communion

Jesus gave us the practice of Communion when He was with His disciples. Here is one of the records of the event from scripture:

> And he said to them, "I have eagerly desired to eat this Passover with you before I suffer. For I tell you, I will not eat it again until it finds fulfillment in the kingdom of God."
>
> After taking the cup, he gave thanks and said, "Take this and divide it among you. For I tell you I will not drink again from the fruit of the vine until the kingdom of God comes."
>
> And he took bread, gave thanks and broke it, and gave it to them, saying, "This is my body given for you; do this in remembrance of me."
>
> In the same way, after the supper he took the cup, saying, "This cup is the new covenant in my blood, which is poured out for you. *Luke 22:15–20*

The early church, starting with the disciples, practiced taking Communion together. The Apostle Paul gives some helpful instructions when taking Communion together as a church or a family

> For I received from the Lord what I also passed on to you: The Lord Jesus, on the night he was betrayed, took bread, and when he had given thanks, he broke it and said, "This is my body, which is for you; do this in remembrance of me." In the same way, after supper he took the cup, saying, "This cup is the new covenant in my blood; do this, whenever you drink it, in remembrance of me." For whenever you eat this bread and drink this cup, you proclaim the Lord's death until he comes.

How Else Will They Know

*So then, whoever eats the bread or drinks the cup of the Lord in
an unworthy manner will be guilty of sinning against the body
and blood of the Lord. Everyone ought to examine themselves
before they eat of the bread and drink from the cup. For those
who eat and drink without discerning the body of Christ eat and
drink judgment on themselves. That is why many among you
are weak and sick, and a number of you have fallen asleep.*
1 Corinthians 11:23–30

According to God's Word, there are a few restrictions on taking
communion. First, communion is for believers. We discussed this in the
chapter, but it's important to mention this again. If you or your children
have not yet placed their faith in Jesus as Rescuer and Leader, then do
not take communion. There are strict warnings in this passage.

Secondly, this passage teaches that we are to "examine" ourselves
BEFORE eating the bread and drinking the juice. That is part of the
purpose of communion - to restore yourself to a right relationship to
God by identifying and confessing your sin to Him. By remembering
Jesus' sacrifice, it gives great motivation to "come clean" to God with
whatever sin has crept into your life. As you lead communion, give
everyone time to reflect on their relationship with God, and to confess
any sin they need to prior to taking the elements.

Once this has been done, remind them of what Jesus said in the first
passage. The bread represents His body that was broken for us. Ask
people to think about the bodily sacrifice of Jesus as they eat their
bread. The juice represents Jesus' blood that was shed for our
forgiveness. Ask people to think about the sacrifice of Jesus on the
cross as they drink the juice. Be sure to encourage them to thank Jesus
for what He did for them.

It is fitting to pray as you finish taking communion, expressing your own
gratitude and love for God for what He has done!

How Else Will They Know

Appendix D

Telling Your Story

If you came to faith in Jesus as an adult, this is a helpful outline to craft your story. Think about Your Story in terms of four essential sections

Section #1: Describe what life was like before you accepted Christ:

What was a deep inner need in your life before you met Christ?

Give some examples of how you tried to fulfill that need with other solutions.

Section #2: Explain how you began a relationship with Christ

Describe the circumstances that caused you to consider Christ.

State how you trusted Christ, briefly including the good news.

Section #3: Describe what life is like now that you have Christ in your life

Give an example of how Christ met or is currently meeting your inner needs.

End with a statement to the effect that you know that you have eternal life.

Section #4: Close by asking them a thought-provoking question

Have you had a similar experience?

Will you tell me about your spiritual story?

Where are you in your spiritual journey?

Who is Jesus to you personally?

How Else Will They Know

If you came to faith in Jesus as a child, strayed away from following Christ, and have since renewed your commitment to Christ, you may find this format helpful:

Section #1: Describe what life was like <u>before</u> your deeper commitment

What was a deep inner need you were trying to fill?

Give some examples of how you tried to fulfill that need with other solutions.

Section #2: Explain <u>how</u> you renewed your relationship with Christ

Describe the situation that caused you to make a deeper commitment to Christ.

Tell about your conversion - how you trusted Christ, briefly adding the good news

Section #3 & #4 - Same as above

How Else Will They Know

Tips for telling Your Story well:

- Practice saying your story in 3-5 minutes
- Avoid dogmatic statements like "you ought', 'you better' and 'you should'
- Avoid mystical statements like "God spoke to me" or describing questionable "signs"
- Avoid arguments by steering clear of controversy or side issues
- Avoid unnecessary details
- Avoid 'churchy' or theological words
- Avoid using 'you', by using 'me' and 'I'. This is YOUR story!

How Else Will They Know

Coaching Questions

Relationship with God:

- What is your relationship with God like currently?
- Are you spending time with God privately?
- When do you feel close to God?
- How does that compliment or conflict with your faith?
- Is there something getting in the way of following Christ?
- What did you learn about God from this experience?
- Are you discovering more of God's purpose for your life?

Relationship with Yourself:

- What did you learn about yourself from this experience?
- How have you felt lately?
- How would you describe your emotional health?
- Is there anything causing you stress?
- What has encouraged you lately?
- What wins can we celebrate together?
- What, if anything, would you change in your life right now? In yourself?
- How can you learn more about what you are interested in? What resources are available to you?
- What do you perceive as your areas of strength? Of weakness?

Relationship with Me:

- How can I serve you better?
- Is there anything that I do that you wish I would change?
- What do you enjoy doing together?

How Else Will They Know

<u>Relationship with Others</u>:

- How do you think that went?
- Do you have someone you can be completely honest with?
- How can you get honest feedback?
- Who needs more of your attention?
- How are you a blessing to others? How could you be?

<u>Wrapping up</u>:

- What other things would you like to talk about that I have not asked you about?
- What decisions are you facing?
- What is one issue that you would like prayer for?

How Else Will They Know

Mercy Ministries

The following are a few of the distinctly Christian and non-denominational ministries that are doing excellent work in meeting the needs of the less fortunate in the name of Jesus. Each of these ministries hold to strict financial accountability and are regarded to have financial integrity.

Holt International

holtinternational.org/

World Vision International

worldvision.org/

Samaritan's Purse International Relief

samaritanspurse.org/

Compassion International, Inc.

compassion.com/

How Else Will They Know

Appendix G

Attributes of God

Pre-existent God is self-caused (*causa sui*) and self-existent. Nothing and no one created God.

> Exodus 3:14; Exodus 6:3

Immutability God, in His nature, attributes, and will, is exempt from change.

> Psalm 102:27; Malachi 3:6; James 1:17

Perfect God possesses quantitative completeness and qualitative excellence.

> Matthew 5:48; Psalm 18:30

Infinity God is subject to no limitations except self-limitations.

> Psalm 145:3; Job 11:7,9; Isaiah 66:1; I Kings 8:27; Romans 11:33

Eternal God's nature is without beginning or end.

> Psalm 90:2; Psalm 102:27; 1 Timothy 1:17; 1 Timothy 6:16; Revelation 1:8

Greatness God is without end, is subject to no limitation of space.

> 1 Kings. 8:27; Romans 8:39

Omnipresence God is present, in the totality of His presence, throughout the universe, at all times.

> Psalm 139:7; Jeremiah 23:23-24; Acts 17:27-28

How Else Will They Know

Omniscience   God is all knowing.

>   Matthew 10:29; Acts 15:8; Psalm 139:2; Matthew 6:8; Isaiah 46:9-10; Isaiah 44:28; 1 Samuel 23:12; Acts 15:18; Hebrews 4:13

Wise   God's choice of that which is always best.

>   Job 9:4; Job 12:13; Psalm 104:24; Proverbs 2:5-7; Romans 16:27

Faithful   God is always true to His word and He is Himself Truth and, therefore, the standard of truth.

>   Deuteronomy 32:4; Jeremiah 10:10-11; Lamentations 3:22-23; John 17:3; Titus 1: 2; Hebrews 6:18; Revelation 3:14

Love   God is eternally self-giving.

>   Zeph. 3:17-18; John 3:16; John 17:24; John 4:8

Goodness   God is the perfection of good.

>   Psalm 34:8; Psalm 100:5; Psalm 106:1; Luke 18:19

Gracious, merciful, patient   Mercy is God's expression of goodness in His not giving us our due punishment; Grace is God's pity and goodness expressed toward those in distress; patience is the expression of God's goodness in withholding due punishment over a period of time.

>   Exodus 34:6-7; Psalm 103:13; Isaiah 30:18; Isaiah 60:10; Ephesians 2:8-9; Titus 3:5

Holy   The attribute by which God eternally wills and maintains His own moral excellence and, as well, is that attribute by which God is separated from all other entities as transcendent.

>   Exodus 15:11; Isaiah 6:3; Revelation 4:8

How Else Will They Know

Righteous/Just   God always does what is right and He is himself the standard of righteousness and justice.

> Genesis 18.25; Deuteronomy 32:4; Psalm 19:8; Isaiah 45:19; Romans 3:25-26

Jealous   God always acts to defend His own honor.

> Exodus 20:5; Isaiah 48:11

Wrathful   God has perfect hatred for all sin.

> Exodus 32:9-10; Deuteronomy 9:7-8; John 3:36; Romans 1:18

Sovereign   God rules perfectly and without limitation over all the universe.

> Psalm 59:13; Psalm 115:3; Isaiah 40:15; Daniel 2:21; 1 Timothy 6:15; Revelation 19:16

How Else Will They Know

PLACE Ministries

Download the free Spiritual Gift Assessment or Personality Type Assessment App from Place Ministries from the Google Play store or the Apple Store:

mySpiritualGifts   myPersonality

MDC Today Foundation, Inc.   MDC Today Foundation, Inc.

How Else Will They Know

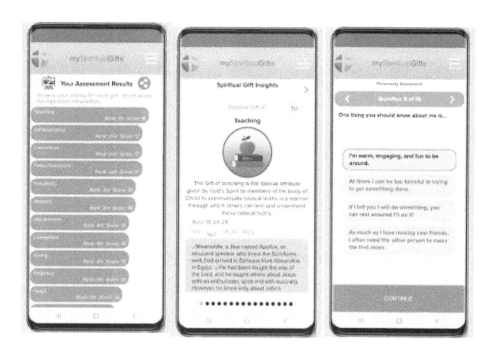

For other free resources, or to take the full PLACE assessment, go to https://placeministries.org/online-store/

How Else Will They Know

Appendix I

30 Family Fun Ideas

1. Take a walk
2. Build a "pillow fort"
3. Movie night (with snacks of course)
4. Throw a frisbee, or frisbee golf
5. Bake cookies together
6. Do a family puzzle
7. Build something out of Legos
8. Play hide and seek (try it with a blanket over the "seekers" head)
9. Play in the snow
10. Play in the rain
11. Look at Christmas lights
12. Play a multiplayer video game
13. Make silly videos (and if you are brave, post one)
14. Play "Minute to Win it" games
15. Have a family sleepover
16. Play a board game
17. Play with their toys with them
18. Dress up and have a father/daughter or mother/son dance
19. Family game of basketball, soccer, badminton, or a sport you all enjoy
20. Give each child the same amount of money to spend at a store

How Else Will They Know

21. Play "twenty questions" to see if you can guess what one person is thinking about
22. Draw pictures, paint, or make something with clay
23. Watch family videos
24. Look at old pictures
25. Take turn telling stories you make up
26. Water fight
27. Go to the park
28. Use one door frame measure and mark their height as they grow
29. Blow bubbles
30. Take your child on a date, letting them pick what you do

What other fun things does your family like to do together?

How Else Will They Know

Appendix J

Family Prayer Journal

Our faith grows as we see God answer prayer. Keeping a simple journal like this will help you see the faithfulness of God as He answers prayers over time. Be aware that God does not always answer prayers the way we think He will. Celebrate together when God does answer your prayers.

Specific Request	Date Requested	God's Answer

How Else Will They Know

Appendix K

Historical Christian Figures

A Chance to Die: The Life and Legacy of Amy Carmichael, Elisabeth Elliot, Revell, 2005

The Autobiography of George Muller, George Müller, Whitaker House, 1996

End of the Spear: When Two Worlds Collide, One Family Faces Its Ultimate Challenge, Steve Saint, Tyndale House Publishers, 2007

Evidence Not Seen: A Woman's Miraculous Faith in the Jungles of World War II, Darlene Deibler Rose,   Harper Collins, 1990

The Heavenly Man: The Remarkable True Story of Chinese Christian Brother Yun, Piquant Editions Limited, m 2003

Jesus Freaks: Stories of Those Who Stood for Jesus, D.C. Talk and Voice of the Martyrs, Bethany House Publishers, 1999.

"Men of Faith" Series, multiple volumes, Bethany House Publishers

The New Foxe's Book of Martyrs, John Foxe, Bridge-Logos, Inc., 1997

Oswald Chambers: Abandoned to God, Oswald Chambers and David McCasland, Billy Graham Evangelistic Association, 1997

Then Sings my Soul: 150 of the World's Greatest Hymn Stories, Robert J. Morgan, Thomas Nelson Publishers, 2003.

How Else Will They Know

Appendix L

Family Devotional Resources

The Beginner's Bible (Best used for Pre-k)

The Action Bible (Best used for Elementary and Middle School ages)

Feeding Your Soul: A Quiet Time Handbook, Jean Fleming, NavPress

The Search for Significance, Robert S. McGee, Thomas Nelson Publishing, 2003

The Purpose Driven Life, Rick Warren,

New Morning Mercies: A Daily Gospel Devotional, Paul David Tripp, paultripp.com

My Utmost for His Highest, Oswald Chambers,

How Else Will They Know

ABOUT THE AUTHOR

Rod Zwemke is a graduate from Georgia Institute of Technology with a Bachelor's degree in Mechanical Engineering. A week after graduation, he married his wife, Gabrian to whom he has been married 26 years. Together they have raised three children, Addison, Dane, and Shea, two of which are now grown.

Six years into Rod's engineering career, God called them to ministry. He served on a large church staff in the areas of evangelism and discipleship for the next five years. He also completed his Masters of Divinity from New Orleans Theological Seminary during this time. While their children were young, they followed God's lead to plant Crossroads Church in Jefferson, Georgia. Rod has been the lead pastor there since then. The whole family has played a role in seeing God establish and use this church to impact lives for Christ. Gabrian has served in a variety of roles over the years and all three of his children continue to serve the local church.

Rod has a heart for seeing disciples, small groups and churches multiplied to reach the world for Christ. Crossroads Church helped start Refuge Church in 2019. Rod has served in leadership roles at a regional level in the area of church planting. He is a trainer for Impact Ministries that "exists to inspire people and churches to be and build disciples of Jesus Christ."

Rod Zwemke
Lead Pastor/Trainer